Healthy Heart

·COOKBOOK·

LOW FAT LOW CHOLESTEROL RECIPES

Tarla Dalal

· INDIA'S #1 COOKERY AUTHOR ·

SANJAY & CO.

MUMBAI

❧ Cook Books by Tarla Dalal ❧

INDIAN COOKING
Tava Cooking
Rotis & Subzis
Desi Khana
The Complete Gujarati Cook Book
Mithai
Chaat
Achaar aur Parathe
The Rajasthani Cookbook
Swadisht Subzian
Punjabi Khana
Mughlai Khana
South Indian Recipes

TOTAL HEALTH
Low Calorie Healthy Cooking
Pregnancy Cookbook
Baby and Toddler Cookbook
Cooking with 1 Teaspoon of Oil
Home Remedies
Delicious Diabetic Recipes
Fast Foods Made Healthy
Healthy Soups & Salads
Healthy Breakfast
Calcium Rich Recipes
Healthy Heart Cook Book
Forever Young Diet
Healthy Snacks
Iron Rich Recipes
Healthy Juices
Low Cholesterol Recipes
Good Food for Diabetes
Healthy Subzis
Healthy Snacks for Kids

WESTERN COOKING
The Complete Italian Cookbook
The Chocolate Cookbook
Eggless Desserts
Mocktails & Snacks
Thai Cooking
Soups & Salads
Mexican Cooking
Chinese Cooking
Easy Chinese Cooking
Sizzlers & Barbeques
Cakes & Pastries
Party Drinks
Wraps & Rolls

High Blood Pressure Cook Book
Low Calorie Sweets
Nutritious Recipes for Pregnancy
Diabetic Snacks
Zero Oil Rotis & Subzis
Zero Oil Soups, Salads & Snacks
Zero Oil Dal & Chawal
Acidity Cook Book
Growing Kids Cookbook
Soya Rotis & Subzis
Cooking with Sprouts
Exotic Diabetic Cooking - Part 1
Healthy Diabetic Cooking
Protein Rich Recipes
Eat Well Stay Well
Weight Loss after Pregnancy
100 Calorie Snacks
Top 10 Healthy Foods [New]
Healthy Starters [New]

MINI SERIES
Cooking Under 10 minutes
Pizzas and Pasta
Fun Food for Children
Roz ka Khana
Idlis & Dosas
Microwave Desi Khana
Paneer
Parathas
Chawal
Dals
Sandwiches
Quick Cooking
Curries & Kadhis
Chinese Recipes
Jain Desi Khana
7 Dinner Menus
Jain International Recipes
Punjabi Subzis
Chips & Dips

Corn
Microwave Subzis
Baked Dishes
Stir-Fry
Potatoes
Recipes Using Leftovers
Noodles
Lebenese
Cook Book for Two's
Know your Dals & Pulses
Fruit & Vegetable Carving
Know your Spices
Know your Flours
Popular Restaurant Gravies
Know Your Green Leafy Vegetables
Paneer Snacks
Pressure Cooker Recipes
Faraal Foods for Fasting Days
Finger Foods for Kids [New]
Microwave Desi Khana - Part II [New]

GENERAL COOKING
Exciting Vegetarian Cooking
Microwave Recipes
Saatvik Khana
The Pleasures of Vegetarian Cooking
The Delights of Vegetarian Cooking
The Joys of Vegetarian Cooking
Cooking with Kids
Snacks Under 10 Minutes
Ice-Cream & Frozen Desserts
Desserts Under 10 Minutes
Entertaining
Microwave Snacks & Desserts
Kebabs & Tikkis
Non-fried Snacks
Mumbai's Roadside Snacks
Tiffin Treats for Kids [New]

Recipe Research & Production Design	Nutritionist	Photography	Printed by
Pinky Dixit	Nisha Katira	Rajeev Asgaonkar	Minal Sales Agencies, Mumbai.
Pradnya Sundararaj	**Copy Editor**	**Design**	
Arati Fedane	Urvashi Srivastava	Satyamangal Rege	

Fourth Printing : 2011

ISBN : 978-8-186469-82-8

Price: Rs. 299/-

Published & Distributed by :

SANJAY & COMPANY

353/A-1, Shah & Nahar Industrial Estate, Dhanraj Mill Compound, Lower Parel (W), Mumbai - 400 013. INDIA.
Tel. : (91-22) 4345 2400
Fax : (91-22) 2496 5876

For books, Membership on **tarladalal.com**, Subscription for **Cooking & More** and Recipe queries
Timing : 9.30 a.m. to 6.00 p.m., Monday to Friday, 9.30 a.m. to 1.00 p.m. Saturday
Contact : Tel. : (91-22) 4345 2400 • Fax : (91-22) 2496 5876
E-mail : ravindra@tarladalal.com • sanjay@tarladalal.com

✒ Introduction ✒

Dear Friends,

All the food that we eat affects the health of our heart.

Healthy Heart Cookbook is our 11th title in the **TOTAL HEALTH SERIES**, after many successful best sellers like Cooking with 1 Teaspoon of Oil, Delicious Diabetic Recipes and Pregnancy Cookbook among others.

Consisting of 78 appetizing recipes from different world cuisines, all the recipes have been *tested and tasted* using minimal amount of oil and are innovative, yet simple and easy to cook. My team of qualified nutritionists have analyzed each recipe for its nutritional value to ensure that they not only please your palate but also maintain your cholesterol levels.

Also included is a wealth of information on eating right for a healthy heart, tips on simple ways to add more fibre and decrease fat, salt and sugar content in your diet....the four most important points to be taken care while planning recipes for a healthy heart.

We could not have put this book together without the guidance of an eminent cardiologist **Dr. Dhanashri Chonkar**. All the recipes and contents were compiled under her watchful eye, meticulously planning calorie-counted meal plans at the end of the book.

Tasty, nutritious 'cooked-at-home' meals are a sound investment in your health and that of your family's too. This book is all about eating well, which means eating foods that are good for you and, even more importantly, *enjoying* what you eat.

Happy and Healthy Cooking!!

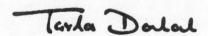

Foreward

Dear Friends,

An Ounce of Prevention Equals a Pound of Cure!

A healthy heart is a result of a healthy lifestyle. Healthy eating, moderate exercise and a stress free environment is an ideal way to keep our health in optimum condition.

As a Cardiologist, I often have to do more than recommend the necessary medication to my patients. More often than not, it's changing a lifestyle in order to improve the person's health.

As heart disease has many causative factors like heredity, hypertension, diabetes mellitus, dyslipidemia (high LDL cholesterol with low HDL cholesterol), coupled with other habits like smoking, sedentary lifestyle, improper diet and mental stress, the problem often gets escalated beyond control.

Most of these can be corrected by a *holistic* approach and a healthy heart diet to watch our cholesterol and triglyceride levels. *"HEALTHY HEART COOKBOOK"* offers you many mouth-watering food choices that will leave you feeling full and satisfied…and not like you're on a deprivation diet.

Also included are *Health Heart Menus* with their caloric, fat and fibre count to help plan your meals. You will also learn about recommended servings and sizes for each food group and discover how easy and fun it is to combine a wide variety of foods to create a heart-friendly diet.

If you were one of those people who thought "nutritious" and "delicious" diet couldn't mix, you're in for a happy surprise! Because that's just what this book is all about…tasty, healthy, simple recipes that you and your family will love.

Regards,

Dr. Dhanashri Chonkar
(Consulting Physician & Cardiologist)

Index

❧ Recipe Index ❧

"The thousand mysteries around us would not trouble but interest us, if only we had cheerful, healthy hearts."
Nietzsche

From the moment it begins beating, until the moment it stops, the human heart works tirelessly. In an average lifetime, the heart beats more than two and a half billion times, without ever pausing to rest. Like a pumping machine, the heart provides the power needed for life.

How Our Heart Functions

The heart is actually a muscle about the size of a clenched fist. It is located in the centre of the chest and tilted a little towards the left. It is the heart that is mainly responsible for nourishing the organs with blood, oxygen and nutrients, through the blood vessels.

The heart is divided into 2 major parts, the left and the right, which work as two pumps. The left side of the heart receives oxygen rich blood from lungs and pumps it to all parts of the body through blood vessels called arteries. The right side of the heart receives the used up (deoxygenated) blood returning from the organs of the body through blood vessels called veins and pumps it to the lungs for purification. The heart then collects the oxygen-enriched blood from the lungs and pumps it to the tissues of the entire body via its left side to continue the cycle of blood circulation in our body.

Like all other organs in the body, the heart too needs oxygen-rich blood to perform all its functions and oxygen-depleted blood must be carried away. For its own oxygen and nutrients, it depends upon the three major arteries called the **"Coronary Arteries"**. Excessive deposition of fat in any of these three arteries leads to the formation of a plaque (a thick, waxy, yellowish fatty substance) which narrows down the blood supply to the heart. If the blood flow is partially restricted, the heart muscle doesn't get enough oxygen, which leads to discomfort and pain in the chest, giddiness as well as pain in the hands and back. It may be accompanied by shortness of breath, sweating and nausea. Medication can be administered to dilate the arteries, which helps to relieve this discomfort immediately.

The problem multiplies when the fat deposition is so high that it forms a clot in the artery already filled with plaque. This results in a *complete blockage* of blood flow to the heart stopping its normal functioning and is named as **HEART ATTACK**.

This explains that the heart is such an important and precious organ that it becomes imperative to ensure a healthy heart and minimise the risk of heart disease. Special attention needs to be paid to nourishing this all-important organ throughout our life and treating it with respect.

Causes of Heart Diseases

There are many factors that can be a risk for your heart and lead to heart disease. They may act individually or jointly in the progression of heart disease.

Some factors, such as smoking, sedentary lifestyle and improper eating habits are within your power to control. Others, such as a family history of heart disease, age and gender factors are risk that we have to be aware of.

However, one thing is certain, by working to eliminate these risk factors that are controllable and by adopting a healthier lifestyle in general, you can greatly reduce your risk for heart disease. Listed below are the most important causes of heart disease.

Heredity: Heredity is one of the most important factors that leads to heart problems. A person with a family history of heart disease is at a higher risk of having heart problems at some stage in life. This does not mean that all persons with a family history of heart disease will definitely have heart attacks. With proper diet control and a sensible exercise regime, the risk factor can be reduced.

Sedentary Lifestyle: An inactive lifestyle leads to obesity and also decreases the HDL levels that help to remove excess cholesterol from our blood. People who have a very sedentary lifestyles are 3 times more likely to have a heart attack than those with active lifestyles.

Obesity: Excessive fat deposition is the root cause of obesity and most obese individuals are prone to complications of the heart. It is also proven that people who have high fat deposits on their abdomen (*apple shaped obesity*) have a higher risk of developing heart disease than those who have more fat deposits on their hips or thighs (*pear shaped obesity*). Most doctors take into account *waist-to-hip ratio (WHR)* in determining how prone the person is to have heart problems. Dividing the waist measurement by the hip measurement in inches determines this ratio. Men who have a *WHR* greater than 0.9 and women who have a *WHR* greater than 0.85 are more prone to heart disease. (If a person's waist measures 44 inches in circumference and the hips measure 40 inches in circumference the waist-to-hip ratio (WHR) is 1.1.)

Improper Eating Habits: Improper eating habits like excessive consumption of fat and sugar are a ladder to obesity which in turn can cause heart disease. Avoiding fibre rich fruits, vegetables and whole grains like wheat, jowar etc. and replacing them with refined foods are also unhealthy eating habits. The reason being fibre is necessary to increase the HDL levels and decrease the LDL levels to protect the heart. Refer to page 14, for more information on HDL and LDL levels.

Age: The risk of heart disease increases with age, peaking at middle age around 50 to 55 years. It is advisable to be cautious about your dietary patterns as the incidence of heart disease increases by approx. 5% every 5 years after the age of 35.

Gender: Men are said to be at a greater risk than women are, in developing heart disease, especially over 45 years of age. Amongst women, post menopausal women are at a higher risk, as a decline in the hormone estrogen leads to a decrease in HDL and an increase in LDL levels. Hence women under the age of 55 are at least risk as they are pre-menopousal.

Smoking and Tobacco: People who smoke and chew or sniff tobacco are more susceptible to heart disease as the nicotine in the tobacco lowers HDL levels and also narrows the arteries, thus obstructing the flow of oxygen and nutrients to the heart. Passive smoking for a prolonged period has also been proven to be a cause of heart disease.

Facts about Fat

Very commonly, we all come across the words Cholesterol, Triglyceride, good fat, bad fat in relation to heart disease. So, let's understand each of these in detail.

Is all fat bad?

In today's society, "fat" seems to have become a nasty word though all the fat in the blood is not bad. In fact, fats are the most concentrated source of energy in our diet that makes us feel satiated for longer periods of time. However, it is crucial to maintain only the minimum level of fat in our body to have a good health for lifetime.

What is cholesterol?

Cholesterol is a thick fatty substance present in our blood. It helps in the formation membranes (that cover our cells) and produces certain essential hormones and vitamin D.

Where does cholesterol come from?

Cholesterol is formed in 2 ways-
In the body, blood cholesterol is made in the liver, which produces all the cholesterol our body needs.
Dietary cholesterol comes from the foods we eat.

Which foods are rich sources of cholesterol?

Animal foods like meats, full fat dairy products, egg yolks, poultry and fish are all high in cholesterol. Plants foods like vegetables, fruits, grains and cereals do not have any dietary cholesterol. **Foods like ghee, butter and cream do not contain cholesterol but when consumed, the saturated fats present in them have the capacity to get converted to cholesterol in the body and raise our blood cholestrol levels.**

What happens when we overeat cholesterol rich foods?

When we overeat high cholesterol foods, its level in the blood rises up above the normal limits leading to its deposition in the arteries which is the root cause of most heart related ailment.

Is all cholesterol in our body bad?

No, not all cholesterol is bad. However, very few people know that some amount of cholesterol is essential for our body. Some amount is important as it forms a protective sheath around the nerves and helps in the production of vital hormones and vitamin D.

What is the connection between cholesterol and lipoproteins?

Like oil and water, cholesterol and blood do not mix. Cholesterol has to be circulated in the blood through carriers viz. lipoproteins. The two types of lipoprotein, which need to be focused on are **HDL** (High Density Lipoprotein) and **LDL** (Low Density Lipoprotein).

What is HDL (High Density Lipoprotein) cholesterol?

HDL is the **good cholesterol** as it carries excess cholesterol in the blood back to the liver for recycling thus avoiding its deposition in the arteries which is why it is called good cholesterol. *So a high level of HDL in the blood protects us from heart diseases while a low HDL level increases the risk of heart disease.*

What is LDL (Low Density Lipoprotein) cholesterol?

LDL carries maximum cholesterol in the blood. It is the **bad cholesterol** as it carries cholesterol to the cells where it gets deposited. If we tend to eat too much of fat, then the liver makes extra LDL cholesterol which gets deposited in the cells and released in the blood which in turn thicken the arteries. *So the lesser the LDL cholesterol, the lesser the risk of heart disease.*

What are triglycerides?

Triglyceride is another type of fat in our blood. It is important to maintain the functioning of all the organs in our body and to maintain normal body temperature.

Where does triglycerides come from?

Like cholesterol, triglycerides are formed partly as a result of metabolism and partly from food.

Which foods are rich sources of triglycerides?

Dairy foods like butter, cream, ghee and non-vegetarian foods are rich sources of triglycerides.

What happens when we overeat foods rich in triglycerides?

When we overeat foods rich in triglyceride, its level in the blood increase and high levels of triglycerides combined with fat deposits in the arteries increases the risk of heart disease.

What levels of fat are good for the heart?

Listed below are the desirable levels of all fats that are good for a healthy heart.

Type of fat	Normal level	Borderline Risk	High Risk
Blood cholesterol	less than 200 mg/dl	201 to 239 mg/dl	more than 240 mg/dl
Blood triglyceride	less than 200 mg/dl	201 to 399 mg/dl	more than 400 mg/dl
Blood LDL	less than130 mg/dl	131 to 160 mg/dl	more than 160 mg/dl
Blood HDL	more than 41 mg/dl	less than 40 mg/dl	less than 20 mg/dl

Here is what these levels are indicative of:

Normal Level : This is the level you need to maintain in you blood for the maintenance of your body cells. There is no risk of heart disease if the cholesterol and triglyceride levels are maintained at this level.

Borderline Risk : This is the level slightly above the normal levels. You need to be cautious, as at this stage you are at slight risk of heart diseases as compared to those who have normal levels. Being cautious about what you eat at this stage with a good exercise regime will definitely help to lower your cholesterol and triglyceride levels and avoid heart diseases too.

High Risk : At this level you are at twice at risk of developing heart problems as compared to those in the borderline risk category. You need to start with a low cholesterol diet along with proper exercise under a doctor's or nutritionist's guidance and check your cholesterol and triglyceride levels every couple of months.

❧ Eating Smart for a Healthy Heart ❧

The foods you eat influence your health, your activity and your energy. As is obvious, your eating habits by far contribute immensely to your fitness. A sensible diet and exercise plan helps keep your heart in optimum condition. Make a *"Heart Healthy"* diet, a part of your daily routine by eating right and reduce the risk of heart disease and prevent further progression in those with existing heart disease.

When you flip through the pages in this book, you will find mouth-watering dishes like Paneer Lababdar, page 83, Penne with Spinach in Low Fat Cheese Sauce, page 110, Custard Fruit Tarts, page 120, and many more… Probably not what you would expect to see in a low fat and low cholesterol menu, right?

The good news is that you can enjoy all your favourite foods by just learning the art of *'heart healthy toggle'*—a switch in the intake of foods you eat. The tables below illustrate what you need to use in your daily food regime, to cook up a hearty meal.

❧ Cereals and Grains ❧

This group includes wheat, jowar, bajra, oats, barley, buckwheat, corn, ragi (nachni), broken wheat (dalia) etc. that form the staple food in most of our households. You can enjoy all these nutritious basic foods in your regular meals, as these do not add up to your daily fat limit. Instead, these foods abound in many vitamins and minerals that your body needs for maintenance of healthy cells.

It is wiser to eat grains with their bran (outer covering of cereals), as bran is a rich source of fibre, which helps to increase the blood HDL levels in the body. For example, whole wheat is a better option as compared to *maida* and semolina. However, if you do consume *maida* occasionally do remember to combine it with equal parts of wheat flour or include other sources of fibre to keep a check on blood cholesterol levels.

See the table on the next page for other healthy cereal choices.

The "Heart-Healthy" **Cereal and Grain Switch to**...*Increase your Fibre and Nutrient Intake*

Instead of	Use this
Maida and semolina	Whole wheat, oats, barley, buckwheat etc.
Polished white rice	Brown rice
White bread	Whole wheat bread
Cream, butter and sugar laden biscuits	Low fat, whole wheat biscuits
Noodles made with plain flour (maida)	Whole wheat noodles and rice noodles
Deep fried puris and tortilla chips	Baked puris and tortilla chips
Buttered and salted popcorn	Fat free unsalted popcorn

Include **6 to 8 servings** of this group in your daily diet.

One serving of cereal is:
1 slice of whole wheat bread (25 gm)
or
2 phulkas (30 gm)
or
1 chapati (25 gm)
or
1 paratha (25 gm)
or
½ cup of any cooked pasta (60 to 80 gm)

Pulses and Legumes

Moong, rajma, toovar dal, chana dal, moath beans, chana, soyabeans etc. are all a part of this group. *These are rich sources of protein, which are essential for maintaining the wear and tear of tissues in the body.* It is necessary to soak, drain and then cook them as soaking releases some anti-nutritional factors like trypsin inhibitors and phytates which decreases the digestibility of protein and hinder with the absorption of other nutrients.

Sprouting the pulses increases their fibre and nutrient (calcium, vitamin C and iron) content too. So, try and include sprouts in any one meal of the day to take advantage of its fibre content. This will help you control the blood cholesterol levels.

Try interesting variations with sprouts like Sprouted Moong and Methi Chilas, page 41, and Tava Sprouts Pulao, page 104 .

It is advisable to use freshly cooked pusles rather than their canned version. This is because the latter is too high in sodium which is unhealthy for the heart as excessive sodium too is known to narrow down the blood flow to the heart.

Soya, the king of pulses, is the highest protein rich pulse. *Apart from being rich in fibre, it has been proven to control the rise in bad cholesterol (LDL).* Most nutritionists that soya be a part of our daily diet rather than an occasional addition to our meals. Apart from soyabeans, the other forms of soya available are soya flour, soya chunks, soya granules, soyabean oil, soya milk and tofu. Soya flour can be mixed into your chapati atta in the proportion of 4 parts of wheat flour (atta) and 1 part of soya flour. Adding anymore soya flour to the wheat flour could impart a bitter aftertaste to your chapatis. You can also add a small quantity of soya flour in cutlets or in your regular pancake mixture too.

Soya granules and nuggets can be used to make vegetable dishes, koftas, tikkis and many other healthy dishes in combination with other ingredients. The Chick Pea and Soya Tikkis, page 59, are an excellent example of this. Soya milk is readily available at most grocery stores and can be used instead of regular milk to make tea, coffee and milk shakes too. Tofu , is also known as bean curd and is used extensively in salads, stir fries and curries.

Check the table below for nutritious protein rich foods for a healthy heart.

The "Heart-Healthy" Pulse and Legume Switch…Decrease your Sodium Intake

Instead of	Use this
Sodium rich canned beans	Any freshly cooked pulses preferable sprouted

Having **2 to 3 servings** of this group is sufficient to fulfil your daily needs for protein.

One serving of pulse or legume is:
¼ cup of whole pulses (35 to 40 gm)
or
½ cup of cooked whole pulses (70 to 80 gm)
or
½ cup sprouts (60 to 80 gm)
or
¼ cup of raw dal (30 to 40 gm)

Or
½ cup cooked dal (70 to 80 gm)
or
½ cup of dal flours (40 to 60 gm)

✥ Dairy Products ✥

Dairy products like milk, paneer, curds, cheese, buttermilk, cream cheese, cream, butter and ghee together make up this group. All dairy products contain high amounts of cholesterol and you will be surprised to know that half the calories in milk actually come from saturated fat. This has a tendency to get converted to cholesterol in the body thus raising the blood cholesterol levels. However, to prevent heart disease or maintain blood cholesterol levels, you need not completely go off dairy products.

To help cut down on the fat from dairy products all you have to do is switch to low fat milk and other low fat dairy products. These are equally good sources of protein and calcium with fewer calories and small amounts of fat.

Preparing low fat milk at home does not demand much effort from your side. It is very easy to prepare. All you need to do is boil the milk and skim the fat layer (*malai*) that is formed after it has cooled. Repeat this procedure at least twice or three times to get almost fat free milk. Another easier way to make low fat milk is to mix skim milk powder with water to make milk, curds, low fat paneer etc. as shown on pages 130-132.

The table below is sure to help you make your dairy product selection easier.

The "Heart-Healthy" Dairy Products Switch...Decrease your Fat Intake

Instead of	Use this
Whole milk	Low fat milk / Soya milk
Whole milk curds and buttermilk	Low fat curds and buttermilk
Whole milk paneer	Low fat paneer / Tofu
Full fat cream cheese and cheese	Low fat cream cheese
Fat and sugar laden ice-creams	Low calorie ice-creams
Ghee and butter	Oil (use sparingly)

Include **2 to 3 servings** of dairy products daily to fortify your diet with protein and calcium.

One serving of dairy product is:
1 cup low fat milk (200 ml)
or
1 cup low fat curds (200 ml)
or
½ cup chopped low fat paneer (70 gm).

❧ Fruits and Vegetables ❧

'*An apple a day keeps the doctor away*'... they say. I would say not just apples but other fruits like oranges, guava, peaches, plums and veggies like, cluster beans, cauliflower, cabbage, green peas etc. also aid good health. There is a wide selection in fruits and vegetables to choose from. Include a wide variety of these fruits and vegetables in your diet to increase your intake of fibre. *Fibre is the key to protecting the heart as it not only helps to decrease bad cholesterol but also reduces total cholesterol itself.* Have fruits and vegetables like guava, apple, carrots etc. unpeeled, as most of the fibre is present just beneath the peel.

Fruits and vegetables also abound in vitamins like vitamin A, vitamin C and vitamin E— all three of which decrease the build up of bad cholesterol (LDL) in the body, due to their antioxidant properties.

Try the 'healthy-heart' fruit and vegetable switch as shown below to increase your fibre intake and you are sure to control your blood cholesterol levels.

The "Heart-Healthy" Fruit and Vegetable Switch…Increase your Fibre Intake

Instead of	*Choose*
Calorie dense fruits like mango, chickoo, custard apple and banana	Fibre rich fruits like guava, orange, sweet lime, papaya, apple etc. Do not peel fruits like apple, guava etc.
Starchy vegetables like potato, suran (yam), kand (purple yam) peas, and sweet potato.	Fibre rich vegetables like cluster beans (gavarfali), French beans, green peas, bitter gourd (doodhi / lauki), bitter gourd, (karela) etc.

Strained fruit juices and vegetable soups	Whole fruits and vegetables or unstrained fruit juices and vegetable soups
Sugar and refined flour based desserts like pastries desserts	Fruit based low calorie

By saying instead of starchy fruits and vegetables have other fruits and vegetables we don't mean to completely avoid them. Make them an occasionally used ingredient in your cooking and watch the way you cook them. For example, you can have a potato treat once in a while, but do not fry it. The calories and fat coming from fried potatoes is the actual culprit. Alternatively you can also make healthy creations like Sweet Potato Salad, page 78, by combining it with the fibre rich fruits and vegetables.

When it comes to vegetables for healthy heart, a meal is said to be incomplete without the use of onion and garlic. The sulphur compound is then act as an anticoagulant which helps to decrease the cholesterol levels in the blood trus preventing clot formation. Hence health experts strongly advice to make raw onion and garlic a part of your daily diet. If you are fussy about eating them raw, due to bad breath, cook them with your regular food. However ensure not to overcook them as too much heating leads to loss of sulphur compounds which in reality aid in building a healthy heart.

Fat

Taking care of your heart is probably the single most important thing you can do for your body and using the right kind of cooking medium is an essential part of that care, along with keeping fit.

You eat what the land gives you. Regionally, people cooked in the oil extracted from oil seeds native to their land. Groundnut, mustard, sesame seed oils are all traditionally used cooking mediums - tried and tested by generations of housewives who found them healthy to use for their families. Mustard oil is ideal for pickling because of its natural preservative properties. Sesame oil enhances flavour of Chinese cuisine and regular daily cooking.

families. Mustard oil is ideal for pickling because of its natural preservative properties. Sesame oil enhances flavour of Chinese cuisine and regular daily cooking.

From this wide range of oils, one question that springs in most minds is "Does each of these oils give equal calories?"

Yes, all fats and oils have the same amount of calories, be it ghee, butter, coconut oil or groundnut oil. Low calorie edible oils are a myth.

1 teaspoon of oil and ghee   = 05 gram   =   45 calories

1 tablespoon of oil and ghee = 15 gram   = 135 calories

However, all oils and ghee are not equal in their effect on blood cholesterol and triglyceride levels.

Broadly speaking there are 3 types of fats present in oils and ghee. They are:

SATURATED FATTY ACIDS (SFA) are bad for your heart as they get deposited on the arteries causing blockages. Butter, ghee, hydrogenated Oils (vanaspati), coconut oil, etc. are examples of saturated fatty acids.

POLY-UNSATURATED FATTY ACIDS (PUFA) based oils lower total blood cholesterol, both, the 'good' and the 'bad'. They may cause damage to the arteries of the heart. Safflower oil and sunflower oil are some **PUFA** based oils. However PUFA are Omega 3 and 6 fats and essential for the body. You can obtain these fats by adding small quantities of any one of walnuts, almonds, sunflower seeds, soy products etc. to your daily meals, rather than having it from **PUFA** based oils.

MONO-UNSATURATED FATTY ACIDS (MUFA) MUFA oils lower only the 'bad' or unhealthy blood cholesterol and improve the 'good' and healthy blood cholesterol levels. This helps reduce risk of heart diseases. Olive oil, groundnut oil, sesame oil and mustard oil are **MUFA** based oils.

The table below explains the function of each of these fats in detail.

Type of Fat	Form	Function	Examples
Saturated Fat (SFA)	Solid at room temperature	Increases the bad cholesterol (LDL) and so the risk of heart disease	Butter, cream, ghee, *vanaspati*, palm oil, margarine, coconut oil, dairy products
Monounsaturated Fat (MUFA)	Liquid at room temperature	Protects good cholesterol (HDL) and decreases bad cholesterol (LDL)	Olive oil, groundnut oil, canola oil, mustard oil, sesame oil
Polyunsaturated Fat (PUFA)	Liquid at room temperature	Decreases bad cholesterol (LDL) but also leads to a slight decrease in good cholesterol (HDL)	Sunflower oil, safflower oil, corn oil, soyabean oil

It is clearly evident from the above table that saturated fat increases the risk of heart disease as it has a tendency to get converted to cholesterol in the body. Hence it is advisable for people with high blood cholesterol levels or even heart disease or people desirous of a healthy heart, to avoid the use of ghee, butter etc. *Instead the right choice of oil makes a better cooking medium as it will have very little saturated fat and high content of unsaturated fat.* However, do remember to use this sparingly as well.

It is advisable for healthy individuals to consume no more than 6 teaspoons (30 grams) of oil per day and not more than 3 teaspoons per day for people with high cholesterol levels or heart disease. Another way of keeping a check on the oil consumption is to measure ½ litre of oil (approx. ½ kg.) per person per month.

Now the next question that comes to most minds is " *Which oil is the best?*"

The answer to this is clear as you can see from the above table. Certainly, all the oils mentioned in the MUFA category. Multiple usage of **MUFA** based oils in your diet will ensure all nutrients and antioxidants present in these oils are included in the daily diet of your family.

Olive oil has been considered healthy amongst this category in the West as it blends with their food taste while groundnut oil is a good option for Indian palates. Studies have shown that groundnut oil is just as effective in protecting against heart disease, as is olive oil. This is because it has similar properties and a similar fatty acid composition, as does olive oil. In addition, refined groundnut oil has special properties that slow down the absorption of cholesterol in the blood, and this works beneficially towards improving heart health. Groundnut oil is naturally stable with a high smoking point, ideal as a multi-purpose cooking medium and safe to reuse.

❧ Nuts and Dried Fruits ❧

Until a couple of years back, nuts were always on top of *'avoid list'* for people with heart disease or high blood cholesterol levels. However, current research states that some nuts actually have a cholesterol lowering effect! *Walnuts* particularly have proven to be good for heart. Next in the series are almonds and peanuts… but the exact effect of these two nuts is yet to be discovered.

Though research is still in progress and the exact reason for walnuts being healthy for heart is not very clear, some of the recent discoveries in this area of research has brought a startling fact to the forefront. Alpha linoleic acid, one of the fatty acid components that make up the total fat in walnuts, reduces the tendency to form blood clots and actually regulates a healthy heart beat.

Walnuts are also rich in omega-3 fatty acids (an essential amino acid), arginine (an amino acid, which is necessary of for the body's production of nitric oxide that keeps the lining of the arteries healthy and elastic, allowing proper blood flow to the heart) and magnesium (which is necessary for healthy functioning of the heart). They abound in vitamin E and folic acid too which helps to decrease the and the chances of clot formation too.

While nuts are good for you, they have certain drawbacks too. They are loaded with calories undoubtedly. So, while you should include nuts in a healthy heart diet, they shouldn't be an-add on to your regular diet BUT should substitute some already present source of calories. Otherwise the benefits of eating nuts might be negated by your expanded waistline. Consult your nutritionist to help you plan a healthy diet, as she is the best person to know your physiological status and pattern of eating.

According to the latest research, 2 to 3 walnuts consumed 2 to 3 times a week can help to lower the risk of heart disease and can help to avoid further damage to the heart in people with existing heart problems or high blood cholesterol levels. The best way to add this nut to your diet is to include them in salads, pasta etc. As we have done in the recipe of Sweet Potato Salad, page 78, and Date and Walnut Footballs, page123.

Amongst the dired fruits, dates, figs, and apricots are healthy options as they lend the necessary sweetness to desserts and milkshakes along with fibre which has a helping hand in controlling blood cholesterol levels. Soya Date Cookies, page 125, and Fig and Cardamom

Delight, page 129, are perfect examples of this. However do put on your Chef cap and get ready for a 'Nutty- heart healthy' meal Say "N (o) UT" to heart disease!!

❧ Are all Beverages Healthy for ❧ Your Heart?

❧ Fruit Juices and Milkshakes: Research has proven that fruits and

vegetables are the most likely foods to reduce the risk of heart disease and stroke. Fruits are considered to be on top of the diet list for people with heart problem or high cholesterol problem. They are rich in antioxidants, which prevent the building up of LDL cholesterol in our blood and thus delay damage to the heart. All red and yellow fruits like orange, sweet lime, papaya etc. and citrus fruits like strawberries, lemon, grapefruit etc. are rich sources of this antioxidant. *So, fruit juices are the best beverages to be consumed, especially in comparison to coffee and aerated drinks, provided they are made with minimal amount of sugar or artificial sweeteners.* Also, the juices should not be strained, a common mistake most of us make, as this loses most of the fibre which actually aids in decreasing blood cholesterol levels. So do remember to say an emphatic "No" to strained juices and milkshakes.

For some refreshing combinations, refer to the recipe of Carrot Coriander Juice, page 44, Watermelon and Mint Drink, page 47 etc. For variety, you can opt for thick milkshakes like Golden Glory Frappé, page 46, but remember to use low fat milk and restrict the amount of sugar being used in them.

❧ Vegetable Soups: Soups are also good for heart as they make use of a

wide variety of vegetables, which are again a rich source of antioxidants. On top of the list are vitamin A and C rich capsicum, broccoli, carrots, pumpkin, cabbage, tomatoes and all the dark green leafy vegetables.

However, in our desire to increase flavour, we often make soups unhealthy by using butter, cream, cheese etc. These ingredients are very high in calories, fat and cholesterol and do no good to your body but rather increase your weight. Instead, you should make use of flavourful herbs and spices to prepare delectable soups and salads, which are healthy, tasty and low in calories as I have done in the recipe of Garlic Vegetable Soup, page 48 , Bean and Tomato Soup, page 55 etc.

Alcohol: Any advice about the consumption of alcohol must take into account not only the complex relation between alcohol and cardiovascular disease but also the well-known association of heavy consumption of alcohol with a large number of general health risks. The argument for and against the consumption of alcohol as part of the 'healthy- heart' diet is poised on the brink. There's still a lot that researchers don't know and it is difficult to determine whether the benefits of alcohol outweigh its risks.

The tannin and antioxidants (phenols and flavonoids) which lend wine and beer its colour prevent the build up of LDL cholesterol into its most noxious form and therefore moderate drinking reduces cholesterol build up, or the hardening of the arteries. Alcohol, most importantly, is also known to stimulate the liver to produce HDL cholesterol, which is the good cholesterol and is known to protect against heart disease.

However, while you consider the potential benefits of moderate drinking, don't forget the potential risks as well. High consumption of alcohol has been proven to damage the arteries of the heart, cause hypertension and affect your brain activity too. It also has a tendency to react with certain medication and negate their effect, thus endangering the heart.

Until researchers know more about alcohol's positive effect on heart, your best bet is to drink in moderation… if at all! This could be about 2 drinks per week. If you do drink occasionally, consult your doctor or nutritionist and ask her to make it a part of your meal plan. Don't feel pressured to start drinking, if you are a non-alcoholic.

Alcohol is definitely NOT an alternative to proven methods of reducing the risk of heart disease, so it is advisable to opt for other options such as increased physical activity, avoiding smoking and controlling blood cholesterol levels with a low fat diet.

Carbonated beverages: Carbonated beverages are consumed by one and all and at all times of the day. However, it is advisable for people with high blood cholesterol and heart problems to avoid carbonated beverages, as these provide no real nutrients, but only empty calories, which means they only help in weight gain. For example, one 12-oz bottle of carbonated beverage has approximately 9 teaspoons of sugar.

However, an occasional indulgence could always be compensated for. If you do get tempted to drink an aerated drink, pour it in a small glass and take small sips. Do remember to include the calories consumed here as a part of your meal that day. Try and burn out these calories through your regular exercise of that day. This way you will be able to enjoy your drink and be tuned in to your diet plan as well. Please do remember not make this a habit. Stay with the simple principle of moderation.

Tea and Coffee:

Coffee has been one of the most controversial beverages. Caffeine, the stimulant in it, is known to energize us and keep us alert. But if you have any heart problem or are in the risk group, most doctors recommend avoiding tea or coffee. This is because of strong evidence that caffeine affects the functioning of the heart by increasing its contractions and altering the regularity of heartbeats. Also, coffee has been known for ages to hinder with the absorption of important nutrients like calcium and iron.

Similarly, tea too has tannins, which hinder the absorption of nutrients. On the other hand, tea is also a rich source of antioxidants named *flavonoids*, which prevent the build up of LDL cholesterol into its most deleterious form, thus preventing the hardening of the arteries. However, a word of caution here! This beneficial effect is seen only when tea is consumed without milk and with restricted addition of sugar. Do have your 'cuppa' but here too, "moderation" is the key word.

Fortify your Diet with Fibre

The importance of fibre has already been discussed in the previous pages. To put it simply, fibre is the complex carbohydrate present in foods, which is not digestible by our body. However, it forms an essential part of our daily diet, as it has more than one function contributing to a healthy living style.

A high fibre diet satiates you for a longer time and helps to prevent raised blood cholesterol and triglyceride levels, thus defending your body against the risk of heart disease. Considering these benefits of fibre, you should include **15 to 25 grams of fibre** in your daily diet.

Have a quick look at few helpful ways to enhance your fibre intake and maintain a healthy heart.

🍂 Choose a breakfast containing high fibre foods like bulgur wheat, oats, soya beans, green peas etc. A classic example of this are the Spicy Oat Pancakes, page 42.

🍂 Snack on fruits in between meals as they will satiate you for longer hours and help to control the blood cholesterol levels too.

🍂 Have plenty of vegetables, especially raw vegetables in the form of salads and raitas. Do not peel vegetables and fruits like cucumber, carrots, chickoos. apples etc. as their peels are edible and much of the fibre lies just beneath the peel. Do remember to wash them thoroughly though, or scrape the peel slightly before eating.

🍂 Choose whole-wheat flour chapatis, jowar and bajra rotis, brown bread, whole-wheat noodles, rice noodles as compared to refined flour products like white bread, pastas, biscuits etc. as bran (outer covering of wheat which abounds in fibre) is lost in the processing of these foods.

🍂 Try to use the bran of cereals like wheat, oats and rice in your regular meals. Adding 1 to 2 tablespoons of bran in the *chapati* dough (see Pyaz ki Roti, page 101) or in the vegetable dishes to enrich your daily meals with fibre. Bran is also a good thickening agent and can add low calorie bulk to soups, gravies etc. Bran is easily available at most health food stores and larger grocery stores.

🍂 Make fibre-rich pulses like moong, rajma, soyabean a part of your daily diet. Sprouting the pulses adds on to their fibre content.

🍂 Surrender the Sugar and Salt Habit 🍂

Sugary and salty foods are to be ranked the last in a healthy heart diet due to the high caloric content of sugar and sodium content of salt. You wil be surprised to know that 1 teaspoon of sugar adds on 20 calories to your menu and all the excess calories get stored as fat, which is one of the most common causes of heart disease.

On the other hand, most doctors and nutritionist advise to restrict the consumption of salt as well. This is because very often people with heart disease have sodium retention in the body which is also responsible for narrowing the blood supply to the heart.

Here are some handy hints to give up the sugar and salt habit and eat healthy.

❧ Decreasing the intake of sugar and salt gradually is sure to help you steadily acquire a taste for food with lower quantities of both. Do not stock sugary and salty foods like biscuits, chocolates, mithais, wafers, etc. at home. Instead, stock up your pantry with low fat and low sugar biscuits like Cream Cracker or Marie, basketfuls of fruits, popcorn made with minimal fat, puffed rice, no fat khakhras etc.

❧ Avoid the consumption of alcohol and soft drinks as they abound in sugar.

❧ Sugary foods like cakes, puddings, pies and cookies are also high in fat and cholesterol. It is a wise decision to stay away from these sugar-laden treats. Use complex carbohydrates such as fruits and vegetables to satisfy your sugar craving.

❧ Restrict the consumption of table salt. An easy way to adapt this into your daily life is by removing the salt-shaker from the dining table and replacing it with pepper-shaker. If you must add salt on the table, then avoid it while cooking.

❧ Experiment with herbs. Season foods with tulsi leaves, curry powder, oregano, chilli powder, dill, caraway seeds, cloves, coriander seeds, cumin seeds, ginger, mustard powder, pepper, sesame seeds, lemon juice, garlic, pepper, orange rind etc. as these ingredients tend to cut down the need for salt.

❧ Eat more fresh fruits and vegetables like guava, orange, papaya, peach, chickoo, brinjal, cucumber, french beans, ladies finger etc. which are low in sodium and high in potassium, as this tends to counteract the effects of high sodium levels in the body.

❧ Avoid papads, pickles, canned and preserved foods, salted foods like chips, popcorn, sev., butter, cheese, salted biscuits, bread and ketchups as these have a high sodium content.

❧ Read nutrition labels on packaged foods correctly. Watch out for words like salt, sodium, sodium chloride and MSG (mono sodium glutamate) as all these are sodium compounds which add up to your total sodium intake.

Cooking Healthy at Home

Tasty, nutritious' cooked-at-home' meals can be a nice reward at the end of an active day instead of opting for quick take away meals. By getting organized, filling the shopping cart with wholesome foods and then cooking wholesome low-fat meals in quantity, you'll be making a sound investment in your health and fueling a active lifestyle. The way you cook is just as important as what you choose to eat. The fact is, some cooking methods are better than others for cutting cholesterol, fat and calories while enhancing the nutritional value of your diet. As a rule of thumb, avoid all cooking methods that allow food to cook only in fat. Instead, try some of the following healthy cooking techniques discussed below…

1. Steaming :
Steaming is a fat free method of cooking food, which keeps the natural flavour, colour and texture intact. It involves cooking food in a steamer basket over boiling water. The moist environment prevents the food from drying and hence no oil is required for cooking. Vegetables steamed only for a few minutes (until they are tender but still crisp) will retain more nutrients than those boiled in water for a longer time. Since the food does not come in contact with the water, more vitamins are retained. Try adding herbs to the steaming water to add more flavour to the food.

2. Pressure Cooking:
This is one of the most effective ways of cooking. Food can be pressure cooked without the necessity of adding fat. Also, pressure-cooking decreases the cooking time by half, thereby reducing the loss of nutrients. Pressure cooking traps the steam inside the utensil because of the tight lid and as the pressure builds up, the temperature rises and forces the steam into the food. Season the pressure cooked food with a good combination of spices, to compensate for the flavours usually lent by fat. The dals given in this book are an excellent example of this.

3. Boiling:
Boiling entails cooking the food in hot water over a high flame. Boiling in most households is used as an alternative method to pressure cooking, especially for vegetables. As this method does not make use of oil, it is a healthy option, but it leads to a loss of water-soluble vitamins like vitamins B and C. So if you happen to choose this method of cooking, the best way to preserve these nutrients is

to cook them in a large volume of ready boiling water. This will help to speedup the process of cooking, leaving less time for vegetables to leach out valuable vitamins. The remaining water can be used to make soups, stocks or gravies.

4. Stir-Frying:

Done in a Chinese wok, this method relies on the same principle as sautéing. However, if you do not have a wok, do not panic. Use a broad and flat bottom non-stick pan for stir-frying. It is a technique of browning foods quickly over high heat in a very small amount of hot fat. High temperatures and constant movement of the food keeps it from sticking and burning.

When stir-frying, it is important that:-
- The pan is very hot so that the food browns well without absorbing the fat.
- The pan is shallow and large enough to hold the food without crowding, so that the food browns quickly.
- The food to be cooked is completely dry, to prevent it from stewing.
- Try one of the recipes like Oriental Soya and Babycorn Stir-Fry, page 58, and Cabbage, Carrot and Babycorn Stir-Fry, page 76, and you will discover for yourself that this method is definitely a fat saving one.

5. Baking:

Baking involves the cooking of food by dry heat in an oven. Baking converts the water content of the food into steam, which combines with the dry heat of the oven to cook the food. A word of caution here! Mind you, baking for healthy heart does not include calorie and fat laden cakes, pastries, pies and other desserts. Baking can be made healthy by avoiding the use of fatty ingredients like oil, butter, ghee, nuts, sugar etc. Try the Crunchy Soyabean Snack, page 60. It's nutritious, healthy and also crunchy.

❧ Eating Out Sensibly ❧

Eating a low fat diet and sticking to it is easy at home. The biggest challenge is to overcome the odds and stick to low fat eating, while dining at restaurants or a party. To begin with, this may look like a mammoth task, but once you have learnt the knack of picking healthy and hearty foods, you will enjoy your food without taking off to bad fat budgets, which hike up your cholesterol levels and add to your weight. Try to observe the following suggestions while partying out to have a balanced and healthy diet.

❧ **Snack sensibly before partying / eating out.** Always have a small fibre-rich snack before leaving for a party. Never go to a restaurant or party with an empty stomach as most party dinners start off late. If, by then, your hunger pangs are in an advanced stage, you may tend to '*pig out*' and end up eating food in excess of what you otherwise eat.

❧ **Plan in advance.** *A little planning goes a long way.* If you have a party to attend, plan well in advance. Do not feel shy or hesitate to request the host or chef to tailor make a dish for you. Remember to enjoy small portions of food at the party, but do compensate for this in the next meal and also by exercising.

❧ **Avoid second helpings.** At the restaurant, serve yourself leisurely and only once, as this will help you to know what you are selecting with respect to calories, fibre, fat etc. Your brain takes 10 minutes to register the feeling of fullness, hence take your time to finish the meal. Serve yourself in a medium sized plate so the food does not look less. This will also ensure that you will not pile up loads of food on the plate.

❧ **Salad bars are helpful**. Begin your meal with a bowl of salad. Beware of salad dressings though! Dressings made with mayonnaise, cream, peanuts etc. are highly calorie dense and an absolute 'no-no'. Instead, choose a lemon juice, vinegar based or low fat curd dressings.

❧ **Choose sensibly.**
   a. Choose foods made with low-fat cooking methods like stir-frying, steaming etc. Refer to cooking healthy at home, on page 32.
   b. Avoid the use of butter, margarine, cheese and ghee, as these tend to increase blood cholesterol levels. Apart from visible fat, saturated fats are also hidden in some foods. Coconut is also a very common example of this. Try and choose gravy made without the use of coconut, while dining out.

c. What's food without a dessert, especially when you are eating out! To satisfy your sweet tooth, select a fruit and low fat milk based dessert and enjoy a small portion. Shake a dessert with a fellow diner instead of having a whole portion yourself.

The gist is to enjoy what you eat. Health doesn't need sacrifice, but you do need to remember that good nutrition is just a matter of selecting the "right" foods whether at home or at a restaurant.

Energize with Exercise

Fit in a healthy diet with other heart healthy measures are exercise and weight control and stress management. You may not care about increasing your strength. "Firm abs" may be the last thing on your mind and even if you don't know your biceps from your bicuspids, there's one muscle you should never ignore- your heart. If you want to avoid heart disease— or are recovering from it—a little sweat can work wonders.

It's never too late to begin. Get started now.....

"I am too busy"
"I am too old to start a exercise regime"
"I can't wake up early in the morning" and so on.....
Excuse yourself from these outdated excuses!!

In fact, you are never too old to get started and good work management will definitely permit some time for exercising. Regardless of your age, gender and role in life you can benefit from regular exercise. Here are some overall benefits of a regular exercise regime.

General benefits of exercise
- Good, energetic start to the day
- An active lifestyle
- Weight control
- Less mental stress and 'bye-bye' to depression
- Improved quality of sleep
- Good posture
- Toned muscles
- Improved self image and hence, self esteem
- Decreased susceptibility to diseases

Along with the general benefits of exercise mentioned above, it is a long proven fact that daily physical activity strengthens the muscles of the heart, thus improving the heart's efficiency to pump blood to all parts of the body. An active lifestyle also helps to increase the HDL levels (good cholesterol) and decrease the LDL levels (bad cholesterol), thus decreasing the risk of heart disease further.

Now the question that would spring in most minds is, "Which activity is best for me?"

It is wisest to choose a form of exercise comfortable to your lifestyle. If you have been inactive for a while, you may start with less strenuous activities such as a brisk walk or a swim at a comfortable pace. Beginning at a slow pace will allow you to become fit without straining your body. Once you are in a better shape, you can gradually move to other types of exercise. Feel free to indulge in a game you enjoy, like tennis, badminton etc. It is advisable to plan a regular exercise regime, best suited to your body and lifestyle. Doing so under your doctor's supervision will ensure an effective regime and help to avoid complications. Do remember that your doctor is the best person to confirm your medical fitness and help you choose a form of exercise that is suitable for your activity level, age and general health.

For overall health benefit, experts recommend that you exercise 20 to 30 minutes on all or most days of the week and also spend some time in stretching activity at least twice a week.

Think you don't have time to exercise and stretch? Try the following ideas to ease your problem. You don't have to live at the gym to protect your heart. Instead of thinking in terms of a rigid exercise programme in the morning, you can even try and incorporate it in your day-to-day lifestyle. Remember that muscles used in any activity and at any time of the day contribute to fitness. You can give your heart a boost simply by just working a little more with extra movements and stretching a couple of times as discussed below:

- Taking the stairs instead of an elevator.
- Do household work to fast music. It will ensure that you work quickly thus burning more calories.
- Park the car at the far end of the parking lot and walk to the office or store.
- Schedule stretching and small walks during breaks at work.
- Make more than one trip to the laundry or grocery store as a form of exercise.
- Get off the public transportation a few blocks away from destination.
- Take a brisk walk when you have an urge to snack.

- Wash your car yourself. It's relaxing and also a good form of exercise.
- Take your dog for a walk.

You can stretch:

- Before going to bed.
- Before getting out of bed.
- While talking on phone.
- After sitting or standing for a long time.
- Before and after exercise.

Most people get excited at the thought of an exercise regime initially and do embark on it. However, soon the rigmarole of life catches up and people cannot continue to follow their exercise regime. However, you must remember that the key to a healthy heart fitness for a lifetime is "consistency". It is only when exercise finds a permanent place in your life that you would succeed in achieving your goal…a good overall health, free from any ailment. But do listen to your body, if you find difficulty while exercising, do not hesitate to consult your doctor.

Here are a few tips to help you make exercise a habit….

- Set realistic goals.
- Choose an activity you enjoy like walking, yoga etc. Do consult your doctor before choosing your exercise regime.
- Begin with a slow pace and gradually increase the intensity
- Give your body a chance to adjust to the new routine.
- Don't get discouraged if you don't see immediate results.
- Don't give up if you miss a day due to some unavoidable reason. Get back to the schedule the next day.
- Find a partner for exercising if possible, as it helps in motivation and socialization.

So think positively and start getting fit. It takes time, effort and a little pain but you have everything to gain in return.

"A man hath no better thing under the sun, than to Eat, Drink and to be Merry."

You too can enjoy all these benefits of a wonderful life, all is required is some care, caution and a fitness regime. Gearing up physically and eating a nutritious diet will help you lead a 'heart-healthy' life, reduce feelings of anxiety and keep you out of the doctor's desk. And I am sure by now you have learnt all about a Heart Smart Diet. **For a delicious, 'heart-healthy' meal, check out our recipe section.....** All you need to do is try to make them a regular part of your diet.

Remember, eat right and feel bright.
By doing so, your heart will be healthier
and so will you!

Abbreviations and Standard Measures

The table below lists the abbreviations used in this book:

Abbreviations Used

CHO	Carbohydrates
AMT	Amount
gm	Grams
kcal	Kilocalories
mg	Milligrams
ml	Millilitres

Standard Measures

All recipes and nutritional values are based on standard cup and spoon measures. They are:

1 cup	=	200 ml.
1 tablespoon	=	15 ml.
1 teaspoon	=	5 ml.

Whole Wheat Salad Wrap

Picture on page 111

The whole-wheat salad wrap is rich in vitamin C, calcium, iron and fibre, making a wholesome, satiating snack, from left over chapatis. This dish can be put together quickly, if the hummus has been prepared in advance and refrigerated.

Preparation time : 20 minutes.   *Cooking time : 30 minutes.*   *Makes 4 wraps.*

4 whole wheat chapatis, approx. 200 mm. (8") in diameter

For the hummus
½ cup chick peas (kabuli chana), soaked
1½ teaspoons garlic, chopped
juice of 1 lemon
4 tablespoons low fat curds, page 131
1 teaspoon olive oil or oil
salt to taste

For the salad
½ cup tomatoes, thinly sliced
½ cup spring onions, sliced
½ cup carrot, cut into thin strips
½ cup bean sprouts
1 cup lettuce, shredded
2 tablespoons finely chopped coriander
2 tablespoons finely chopped mint
½ teaspoon roasted cumin (jeera) powder
juice of ½ lemon
1 teaspoon olive oil or oil
salt to taste

For the hummus
1. Soak the chick peas in water for 6 hours making sure that they are covered with water.
2. Cook the chick peas in a pressure cooker. Cool and drain. Keep the drained liquid aside.

3. Add the olive oil, lemon juice, curds, cooked chick peas, garlic, salt and some of the strained water in a blender and blend until smooth. If the mixture is too thick, add 2 to 3 tablespoons of the reserved liquid.
4. Keep refrigerated.

For the salad
1. Combine all the vegetables, bean sprouts and lettuce in a bowl and refrigerate for at least 30 minutes.
2. Just before serving, add the cumin powder, lemon juice, olive oil and salt and mix well.

How to proceed
1. Place one chapati on a clean dry surface.
2. Spread an even layer of hummus on the chapati.
3. Top with a generous portion of salad in the centre of the chapati and roll up tightly.
4. Repeat to make the remaining 3 wraps.
   Serve immediately.

Nutritive values per wrap:

AMT	ENERGY	PROTEIN	CHO	FAT	FIBRE
gm	kcal	gm	gm	gm	gm
120	112	6.0	17.1	2.2	1.7

Handy tip : Approximately ¼ cup of kabulichana (chickpeas) gives you ½ cup of kabuli chana, soaked.

Sprouted Moong and Methi Chilas

Sprouts, a good source of protein, iron and vitamin C, and a great add-on to our daily meals. This is an easy-to-make dish and ensures intake of sprouts for those who do not otherwise like them.

Preparation time : 10 minutes.   Cooking time : 15 minutes.   Makes 4 chilas.

For the chilas
1 cup moong (whole green gram) sprouts
½ cup fenugreek (methi) leaves, chopped
1 tablespoon Bengal gram flour (besan)
3 green chillies
25 mm. (1") piece ginger
salt to taste
1 teaspoon oil for cooking

For the tempering
½ teaspoon cumin seeds (jeera)
2 pinches asafoetida (hing)
1 teaspoon oil

To serve
4 tablespoons carrot garlic chutney, page 66

For the chilas
1. Combine the moong sprouts, green chillies, ginger and ½ cup water and grind into a smooth batter.
2. Add the fenugreek leaves, besan and salt and mix well. Keep aside.

For the tempering
1. Heat the oil, add the cumin seeds and allow the seeds to crackle.
2. Add the asafoetida and mix well.

How to proceed
1. Pour the tempering over the batter and mix well.

2. Heat and grease a non-stick tava (griddle) with a little oil.
3. Pour a ladleful of the batter on the tava and spread it evenly by moving the pan in a circular motion to make a chila with 125 mm(5″) diameter.
4. Drizzle a little oil on the sides and allow it to cook.
5. When the chila is lightly browned, flip to the other side and cook again till it is golden brown in colour.
6. Repeat to make 3 more chilas.
   Serve hot with the carrot garlic chutney.

Nutritive values per chila:

AMT	ENERGY	PROTEIN	CHO	FAT	FIBRE
gm	kcal	gm	gm	gm	gm
36	84	4.5	11.2	2.3	0.8

Spicy Oat Pancakes

These pancakes are made by adding oats to wheat flour, as oats are highly nutritious and filled with cholesterol-fighting soluble fibre. Being extremely satiating, they prevent you from bingeing on junk food. Serve these pancakes hot, along with mint and coriander chutney.

Preparation time : 4 minutes.   *Cooking time : 7 minutes.*   *Makes 4 pancakes.*

¼ cup quick cooking rolled oats
¼ cup jowar flour (white millet flour)
¼ cup wheat flour (gehun ka atta)
¼ cup onions, chopped
¼ cup tomatoes, chopped
2 tablespoons chopped coriander
1 teaspoon ginger-green chilli paste
salt to taste
1 teaspoon oil for cooking

To serve
2 tablespoons coriander garlic chutney, page 70

1. Mix together all the ingredients in a bowl and add enough water to make a thick batter.
2. Grease and heat a non-stick tava (griddle).
3. Spread a layer of the batter to form a pancake of 4 mm. thickness.
4. Cook on both sides till golden brown, using a little oil.
5. Repeat to make 3 more pancakes.
   Serve hot with the coriander garlic chutney.

Nutritive values per pancake:

AMT	ENERGY	PROTEIN	CHO	FAT	FIBRE
gm	kcal	gm	gm	gm	gm
45	81	2.4	13.6	1.9	0.6

Waldorf Open Sandwich

Picture on page 51

Sandwiches make a great start for the day. This can be put together by anyone in no time at all. It requires no cooking and we can soon have a satisfying, delicious, wholesome filler ready. Whole wheat bread, pears and sprouts are the key ingredients in this dish which makes it heart-friendly due to their high fibre content.

Preparation time : 10 minutes.   *No cooking.*   *Makes 2 sandwiches.*

4 slices whole wheat bread

For the salad
¼ cup pears or apples, grated
1 tablespoon finely chopped celery
1 spring onion, finely chopped
½ cup alfalfa sprouts

To be mixed together into a dressing
¼ cup low fat curds, page 131
½ teaspoon prepared mustard paste
salt and pepper to taste

1. Toss the salad ingredients with the dressing.

2. Divide into 2 portions and spread each one on 2 slices of bread.
3. Top with the remaining 2 slices of bread and cut each sandwich into 2 triangles.
   Serve immediately.

Handy tip : Feel free to use beans sprouts instead of alfalfa sprouts.

Nutritive values per sandwich:

AMT	ENERGY	PROTEIN	CHO	FAT	FIBRE
gm	kcal	gm	gm	gm	gm
96	165	8.2	31.5	0.8	1.8

Carrot Coriander Juice

Picture on page 52

This juice is absolutely low in calories and is not strained so as to retain all the fibre in the juice itself. Whole Wheat Salad Wrap, page 39, with this juice makes an ideal breakfast treat that's really rich in fibre.

Preparation time : 5 minutes.   **No cooking.**   **Serves 2.**

2 cups carrots, grated
2 tablespoons chopped coriander
½ teaspoon lemon juice
2 cups water
salt to taste

To serve
8 ice-cubes

1. Blend together the carrots and water in a mixer to get a smooth purée.
2. Add the coriander, lemon juice and salt and serve over ice-cubes.

Nutritive values per serving:

AMT	ENERGY	PROTEIN	CHO	FAT	FIBRE
gm	kcal	gm	gm	gm	gm
62	30	0.6	6.4	0.2	0.8

Tomato Apple Juice

Picture on page 51

An unusual combination, which is a perfect substitute for sugar laden juices during breakfasts. Here, sugar has been completely replaced by just a teaspoon of honey to get the required sweetness, with minimal calories.

Preparation time : 10 minutes.   **No cooking.**   **Serves 2.**

½ cup apple, chopped
1 cup tomatoes, chopped
1 teaspoon honey
4 to 6 ice-cubes

1. Combine all the ingredients in a blender with 1 cup of water and blend till it is smooth.
2. Pour into 2 glasses and serve immediately.

Nutritive values per serving:

AMT	ENERGY	PROTEIN	CHO	FAT	FIBRE
gm	kcal	gm	gm	gm	gm
113	45	0.9	9.9	0.3	1.0

Golden Glory Frappé

This cool refreshing drink is appealing nutritionally as well as visually due to its colour. Nutmeg further adds a touch of flavour to this low fat, high fibre drink. The combination of sweet papaya and honey helps to avoid the use of sugar completely.

Preparation time : 5 minutes.   · **No cooking.**   **Serves 2.**

1½ cups papaya pieces
½ cup apple pieces
¼ cup low fat curds, page 131
a pinch nutmeg (jaiphal) powder
1 teaspoon honey
6 to 8 ice-cubes

1. Combine all the ingredients alongwith 1 cup water and purée till it is smooth.
2. Pour into 2 glasses and serve immediately.

Nutritive values per serving:

AMT	ENERGY	PROTEIN	CHO	FAT	FIBRE
gm	kcal	gm	gm	gm	gm
143	72	1.7	15.9	0.3	1.2

Watermelon and Mint Drink

This quick-to-prepare juice is a wonderfully refreshing energiser. Watermelon, filled with 90% water, is low in fat and the addition of mint gives a perfect lift to the taste of watermelon. Skim milk powder has been used to add protein and calcium to the diet while avoiding the fat.

Preparation time : 5 minutes.　　　*No cooking.*　　　*Makes 3 glasses.*

3 cups watermelon pieces
3 tablespoons skim milk powder
1½ teaspoons sugar
1 tablespoon mint, chopped

1. Blend all the ingredients except the mint in a liquidiser till it is a smooth purée.
2. Add the mint, mix well and serve immediately.

Nutritive values per glass:

AMT	ENERGY	PROTEIN	CHO	FAT	FIBRE
gm	kcal	gm	gm	gm	gm
174	79	4.9	13.9	0.3	0.3

SOUPS

 Garlic Vegetable Soup

This nourishing concoction of vegetables and garlic is thickened using rolled oats. This helps add a creamy texture and also more fibre to this soup.

Preparation time : 10 minutes.   *Cooking time : 15 minutes.*   *Serves 4.*

1 cup mixed vegetables (carrots, French beans, cauliflower, peas, babycorn), finely chopped
¼ cup onions, finely chopped
2 teaspoons garlic, finely chopped
2 tablespoons quick cooking rolled oats
1 teaspoon oil
salt and pepper to taste

For the garnish
2 tablespoons chopped coriander

1. Heat the oil in a non-stick pan, add the onions and garlic and sauté till the onions are translucent.
2. Add the vegetables and sauté for a few minutes.
3. Add 2 cups of water and salt and pepper and allow it to come to a boil and simmer till the vegetables are tender.
4. Add the oats and simmer for another 5 minutes.
    Serve hot garnished with the coriander.

Nutritive values per serving:

AMT	ENERGY	PROTEIN	CHO	FAT	FIBRE
gm	kcal	gm	gm	gm	gm
44	49	1.6	7.5	1.5	0.9

Green Peas and Mint Soup

This unusual combination of green peas and mint may surprise you, but this is one of the most appreciated recipes that I make. And it is so easy to prepare too!! The wealth of this soup lies in the fibre-rich green peas which help to decrease blood cholesterol levels.

Preparation time : 10 minutes.   **Cooking time : 20 minutes.**   **Serves 2.**

¾ cup fresh green peas
¼ cup onions, chopped
1 teaspoon garlic, finely chopped
1 teaspoon oil
salt and pepper to taste

For serving
1 tablespoon finely chopped mint
1 tablespoon grated carrots

1. Heat the oil in a non-stick pan and sauté the onions for a few seconds.
2. Add the garlic and sauté for a few more seconds.
3. Add the peas along with 2 cups of water and salt and bring it to a boil.
4. Simmer till the peas are cooked.
5. Cool and purée in a blender.
6. Reheat, adjust the salt and add the pepper.
   Serve hot topped with the chopped mint and grated carrots.

Nutritive values per serving:

AMT	ENERGY	PROTEIN	CHO	FAT	FIBRE
gm	kcal	gm	gm	gm	gm
79	83	4.1	10.9	2.6	2.3

Makai Shorba

Everyone is sure to relish this tempting, Indian-style corn soup. This refreshing soup is a great energiser and will surely establish your culinary skills.

Serve hot with garlic bread, to make an absolutely low calorie 'hearty' meal.

Preparation time : 5 minutes.   **Cooking time : 15 minutes.**   **Serves 2.**

½ cup sweet corn kernels
¼ cup onions, chopped
1 clove (laung)
25 mm. (1") stick cinnamon (dalchini)
2 peppercorns
1 bay leaf (tejpatta)
2 cloves garlic, sliced
¼ cup carrots, cubed
½ teaspoon crushed coriander (dhania) seeds
¼ teaspoon cumin (jeera) powder
a pinch turmeric powder (haldi)
1 teaspoon oil
salt to taste

To serve
lemon juice
1 tablespoon chopped coriander

1. Heat the oil in a non-stick pan, add the clove, cinnamon, peppercorns, bay leaf, onions and garlic and cook till the onions are translucent.
2. Add the carrots, coriander seeds, cumin powder and turmeric powder and cook for 3 to 4 minutes.
3. Add the corn kernels, 3 cups of water and salt and simmer over a medium flame for 10 to 15 minutes, till the corn is cooked.
4. Cool completely and make a smooth purée in a blender. Transfer back into a pan.
5. Bring to a boil and serve hot with the lemon juice and coriander.

AMT	ENERGY	PROTEIN	CHO	FAT	FIBRE
gm	kcal	gm	gm	gm	gm
63	69	1.5	11.0	2.6	1.1

Miso Soup

A warm accompaniment to Oriental Soya and Baby Corn Stir-fry, page 58, this soup is full of vitamin A, vitamin C, calcium and protein, with extremely low fat content. It's a light yet satiating treat for the heart.

Preparation time : 10 minutes.   **Cooking time : 15 minutes.**   *Serves 4.*

½ cup red pumpkin (kaddu), cubed
½ cup sweet (yellow) corn
¼ cup spring onions, chopped
½ cup carrot, peeled and cubed
½ cup mushrooms, cut into quarters
½ cup spinach (palak), chopped
½ cup low fat paneer (cottage cheese) page 132, cubed
½ tablespoon grated ginger
1 large clove garlic, finely chopped
salt to taste

For serving
1½ teaspoons soya sauce
juice of ½ lemon
pepper to taste

1. Bring 4 cups of water to a boil in a pan and add the ginger and garlic to it.
2. Add the red pumpkin, corn, spring onions and carrot and simmer till the vegetables are almost cooked.
3. Add the mushrooms, spinach, paneer and salt and simmer for 4 to 5 minutes. Serve hot with soya sauce, lemon juice and pepper.

AMT	ENERGY	PROTEIN	CHO	FAT	FIBRE
gm	kcal	gm	gm	gm	gm
73	70	5.5	12.2	0.2	0.9

Carrot and Lentil Soup

This interesting variation makes a great change for your palate. It works effortlessly with onions, garlic and tomatoes in it. The low fat milk in the soup does not add cholesterol to the diet. The protein in the low fat milk complements the protein in the lentils, thus making this a nourishing combination.

Preparation time : 10 minutes.　　　*Cooking time : 20 minutes.*　　*Serves 4.*

1 cup carrots, chopped
½ cup green moong dal (split green gram), soaked for 4 to 6 hours
6 peppercorns
¼ cup onions, sliced
1 teaspoon garlic, chopped
¼ cup tomatoes, chopped
¾ cup low fat milk, page 130
1 teaspoon oil
salt and pepper to taste

1. Heat the oil in anon-stick pan and add the peppercorns, onions and garlic and sauté for 2 to 3 minutes.
2. Add the carrots and tomatoes and sauté for 4 minutes.
3. Add the green moong dal and 1 cup of water and cook till the carrots are tender.
4. Cool the carrot mixture and purée to a smooth paste.
5. Transfer the puréed soup to a pan, add the milk, 1½ cups of water, salt and pepper and allow it to come to a boil.
   Serve hot.

Nutritive values per serving:

AMT	ENERGY	PROTEIN	CHO	FAT	FIBRE
gm	kcal	gm	gm	gm	gm
52	102	6.3	15.6	1.5	0.6

 # *Bean and Tomato Soup*

Protein from black beans as well antioxidants, vitamin A from tomatoes and vitamn C from capsicum, all together work towards maintaining the cells and the lining of the arteries in good health.

Preparation time : 5 minutes.   *Cooking time : 30 minutes.*   *Serves 4.*

½ cup black beans, soaked
1 to 2 bay leaves
½ cup onions, sliced
¼ cup capsicum, chopped
1 teaspoon garlic, chopped
1 cup tomatoes, finely chopped
1 teaspoon oil
salt and pepper to taste

1. Drain out all the water from the beans and add 2 cups of fresh water, salt and bay leaves and pressure cook for 2 to 3 whistles till they are soft. Remove the bay leaves and discard.
2. Heat the oil in a non-stick pan and sauté the onions for a few minutes till they are translucent.
3. Add the capsicum and garlic and sauté for a few more seconds.
4. Add the tomatoes and cook for a few minutes over a slow flame till they soften.
5. Add the beans along with the liquid in which they were cooked and bring to a boil.
6. Simmer for 5 to 7 minutes and season with salt, if required, and pepper. Serve hot.

Handy tip : You can use any choice of beans instead of the black beans. Use rajma, chawli beans etc.

AMT	ENERGY	PROTEIN	CHO	FAT	FIBRE
gm	kcal	gm	gm	gm	gm
74	59	2.7	8.9	1.5	0.9

Cauliflower Soup

A creamy, crunchy soup which is sure to tickle your taste buds. The vitamin A in celery is an antioxidant which helps to keep the lining of the arteries in good health. Being extremely low in fat and free from cholesterol, this delectable soup is a perfect appetizer for those "heart conscious" people.

Preparation time : 10 minutes.   *Cooking time : 15 minutes.*   *Serves 4.*

2 cups cauliflower, chopped
1 cup onions, finely chopped
2 cups low fat milk, page 130
2 tablespoons celery, chopped
1 teaspoon oil
salt and pepper to taste

1. Heat the oil in a non-stick pan and sauté the onions till they are translucent.
2. Add the cauliflower and sauté for another 4 to 5 minutes.
3. Add 2 cups of water and milk and bring to a boil.
4. Season with salt and pepper and simmer till the cauliflower is partially cooked.
5. Cool slightly and blend roughly using a handblender, so the soup looks like a rough purée.
6. Bring the purée to a boil, add the celery and serve hot.

Nutritive values per serving:

AMT	ENERGY	PROTEIN	CHO	FAT	FIBRE
gm	kcal	gm	gm	gm	gm
85	75	5.2	10.4	1.4	0.7

Spinach Soup with Garlic

This nutritious, low fat, low calorie soup is best if you are trying to lose some of those extra pounds. The garlic and onion in the soup aids in decreasing the excessive fat deposition in the arteries.

Preparation time : 15 minutes.   *Cooking time : 15 minutes.*   *Serves 4.*

3 cups spinach (palak), sliced
¾ cup onions, finely chopped
2 teaspoons garlic, chopped
1 teaspoon oil
salt and pepper taste

For serving
toasted whole wheat bread

1. Heat the oil in a non-stick pan, add the onions and garlic and cook till the onions are translucent.
2. Add the spinach and cook over high flame till the spinach turns to a bright green colour.
3. Add 3 cups of cold water and purée the mixture in a blender to a coarse texture.
4. Pour the purée back to the pan, add salt and pepper and allow the soup to come to a boil.
    Serve hot with toasted whole wheat bread.

Nutritive values per serving:

AMT	ENERGY	PROTEIN	CHO	FAT	FIBRE
gm	kcal	gm	gm	gm	gm
77	37	1.3	4.2	1.6	0.5

Oriental Soya and Babycorn Stir-fry

Stir-fries are always on top of my list, when it comes to healthy cooking, to monitor the amount of fat used. I have chosen soya nuggets because of their decreasing nature of LDL (bad) cholesterol and baby corn to give the needed crunch without any amount of fat.

Preparation time : 10 minutes.   *Cooking time : 10 minutes.*   *Serves 2.*

¼ cup soya nuggets
½ cup mushrooms, sliced
½ cup babycorn, sliced and parboiled
¼ cup capsicum, diced
¼ cup spring onion whites, chopped
1 teaspoon, garlic, chopped
1 teaspoon soya sauce
2 tablespoons tomato-chilli sauce
½ cup spring onion greens, chopped
1 teaspoon oil
a pinch sugar
salt to taste

1. Soak the soya nuggets in warm water for 10 to 15 minutes. Drain and squeeze out the water.
2. Heat the oil in a non-stick pan, add the spring onion whites and garlic and cook over high flame till the onions turn golden brown in colour.
3. Add the mushrooms and cook till they are partially cooked.
4. Add the soya nuggets, babycorn, capsicum and cook for 2 minutes.
5. Add the soya sauce, tomato-chilli sauce, sugar and salt and cook for 2 more minutes.
6. Add the spring onion greens and cook for another 1 minute.
   Serve immediately.

AMT	ENERGY	PROTEIN	CHO	FAT	FIBRE
gm	kcal	gm	gm	gm	gm
114	129	6.8	16.9	3.6	2.1

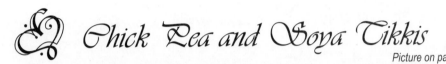

Chick Pea and Soya Tikkis

Picture on page 25

Tikki, a traditional Indian snack is presented with a variation here. The additional soya helps to decrease cholesterol, while the chick peas give the Indian flavour to the dish. The tikkis are made in just 1 teaspoon of oil to add only 20 calories to your diet, instead of adding 80 calories by being deep-fried, thus making the snack healthy for the heart.

Preparation time : 10 minutes.   *Cooking time : 10 minutes.*   *Makes 4 tikkis.*

½ cup chick peas (kabuli chana), boiled and drained
½ cup soya granules
1 tablespoon mint, finely chopped
1 teaspoon green chillies, finely chopped
1 teaspoon ginger, finely chopped
1 teaspoon oil
salt to taste

To serve
2 tablespoons high fibre chutney, page 71

1. Soak the soya nuggets in hot water for 10 to 15 minutes. Drain and squeeze out all the water.
2. Blend together the chick peas, soya nuggets and mint, in a blender to a smooth paste.
3. Add the green chillies, ginger and salt and mix well.
4. Divide the mixture into 4 equal portions and shape into round, flat tikkis.
5. Cook them on a non-stick pan using a little oil till both sides are golden brown.
   Serve hot with the high fibre chutney.

AMT	ENERGY	PROTEIN	CHO	FAT	FIBRE
gm	kcal	gm	gm	gm	gm
26	81	4.8	8.6	3.1	0.7

 # Crunchy Soyabean Snack

This is one of the tastiest low-fat, low-cholesterol snack which requires almost no oil for preparation and is great to munch at any time of the day. You can even add some chilli powder and amchur powder to these to make them more chatpata.

Preparation time : Overnight.   **Baking time : 1 hour.**   **Serves 4.**
Baking Temperature : 140°C (280°F).

½ cup soyabeans
½ teaspoon turmeric powder (haldi)
1 teaspoon salt
oil for greasing

1. Soak the soyabeans in water for 3 hours.
2. Drain out all the water and add the salt and turmeric powder.
3. Mix well and keep refrigerated overnight.
4. Dry the soyabeans on a dry kitchen towel to remove any. excess moisture.
5. Place on a greased baking tray and bake in a pre-heated oven at 140°C (280°F) for 40 to 50 minutes or till the soyabeans are lightly browned and crisp.
6. Cool completely and store in an air-tight container.

Variation : Microwave them in 3 batches for 5 minutes each. These will not brown like the ones cooked in the oven, but are nice and crispy on cooling.

Nutritive values per serving:

AMT	ENERGY	PROTEIN	CHO	FAT	FIBRE
gm	kcal	gm	gm	gm	gm
18	82	7.7	3.7	4.1	0.7

Crunchy Cumin Seed Crackers

These crispy, low fat munchies are made with oats, maize flour and whole-wheat flour instead of refined maida.

These are great to keep in your handbag so that you are prepared when hunger strikes. You can also serve them as an appetizer along with a Garlic Tomato Salsa, page 67.

Preparation time : 10 minutes.   *Baking time : 20 minutes.*   *Makes 30 crackers.*
Baking temperature : 160°C (320°F).

¾ cup whole wheat flour (gehun ka atta)
1½ teaspoons cornflour
2 tablespoons maize flour (makai ka atta)
2 teaspoons skim milk powder
¼ cup quick cooking rolled oats
½ teaspoon cumin seeds (jeera)
1 tablespoon low fat curds, page 131
salt to taste

Other ingredients
1 teaspoon oil for greasing

1. Mix all the ingredients together and add enough water to make a firm dough.
2. Knead the dough gently until smooth.
3. Roll out, using a little whole wheat flour to 2 mm. thickness.
4. Pierce with a fork and cut them into squares that are 50 mm. (2") using a knife.
5. Place on greased baking tray and bake in a pre-heated oven for 20 minutes at 160°C (320°F) or until lightly brown and crisp.
6. Cool and store in an air-tight container.

Nutritive values per cracker:

AMT	ENERGY	PROTEIN	CHO	FAT	FIBRE
gm	kcal	gm	gm	gm	gm
5	18	0.7	3.0	0.3	0.1

Soya Sesame Khakhra

Picture on page 86

These are a crisp, oil-free snack that will keep you going, right up till dinner. This snack abounds in all the nutrients except the fat and also provides the excuse to add methi to your diet.

Preparation time : 10 minutes.   Cooking time : 30 minutes.   Makes 6 khakhras.

½ cup soya flour
¼ cup whole wheat flour (gehun ka atta)
1 teaspoon sesame seeds (til), black and white
salt to taste

1. Sprinkle salt on the methi leaves and keep aside for 5 to 7 minutes.
2. Combine all the ingredients and knead into a firm dough using enough water if required.
3. Keep aside for 10 to 15 minutes and divide the dough into 6 equal portions.
4. Roll out each portion into large circles of 150 mm. (6") in diameter.
5. Cook each one on a non-stick tava (griddle), over a low flame pressing each side with a cloth to make the khakhras crisp.
6. Cool and store in an air-tight container.

AMT	ENERGY	PROTEIN	CHO	FAT	FIBRE
gm	kcal	gm	gm	gm	gm
11	42	3.1	4.4	1.3	0.3

Oat and Raisin Biscuits

Oats are a great substitute for low fibre maida and raisins are the least fat containing dry fruits, making these biscuits healthy and tasty. Raisins also lend their sweetness to the biscuits, reducing the required sugar content.

Preparation time : 15 minutes.   *Baking time : 25 minutes.*   *Makes 9 biscuits.*
Baking temperature : 180°C (360°F).

¾ cup quick cooking rolled oats
¼ cup whole wheat flour (gehun ka atta)
¼ cup raisins (kismis)
2 tablespoons low fat milk, page 130
¼ cup brown sugar
1 tablespoon oil

1. Mix all the ingredients together and divide into 9 equal portions.
2. Grease a baking tray lightly and place a sheet of grease proof paper on top.
3. Place the mixture on the greased and lined baking tray and flatten each round with the back of a fork.
3. Bake in a pre-heated oven for 20 minutes at 180°C (360°F) or until the cookies are baked.
4. Peel them off the baking tray and cool on cooling racks.
5. Store in an air-tight container.

Handy tip : The cookies will appear a little soft when hot, but will get crisp once they cool down to room temperature.

Nutritive values per biscuit:

AMT	ENERGY	PROTEIN	CHO	FAT	FIBRE
gm	kcal	gm	gm	gm	gm
19	78	1.4	13.1	2.2	0.3

Mini Pizzetas

Picture on page 52

Pizzas are usually considered to be calorie-laden. Now, here is a healthy version, made with only 1 teaspoon of cheese per pizza and a whole lot of veggies, yet maintaining the authentic pizza taste.

Preparation time : 10 minutes.   *Baking time : 10 minutes.*   *Makes 4 pizzetas.*
Baking temperature : 200°C (400°F).

4 slices whole wheat bread

To be mixed into a topping
½ cup tomatoes, finely chopped
2 tablespoons finely chopped celery
½ cup spring onions, finely chopped
¼ cup capsicum, finely chopped
½ teaspoon finely chopped garlic
¼ cup crumbled low fat paneer (cottage cheese), page 132
4 teaspoons grated cheese
salt and pepper to taste

1. Spread equal portions of the topping mixture onto each of the 4 slices of bread.
2. Bake them in a pre-heated oven at 200°C (400°F) for 7 to 10 minutes till they are golden brown.
3. Cut each slice into 4 wedges and serve hot.

Nutritive values per pizzeta:

AMT	ENERGY	PROTEIN	CHO	FAT	FIBRE
gm	kcal	gm	gm	gm	gm
60	86	4.9	14.1	1.1	0.7

Soya Bhel

Picture on page 52

*This is a tasty and nutritious variation of the popular Indian snack—
bhelpuri. This recipe has been created to help one adapt the taste of soya
gradually and maintain the cholesterol levels...Veggies like tomatoes,
spring onions and cabbage helps to mask the after taste of soya. Addition
of lemon juice and chilli powder further enhances the flavours.*

Preparation time : a few minutes.   *Cooking time : 5 minutes.*   *Serves 4.*

½ cup soyabeans
¼ teaspoon turmeric powder (haldi)
¼ cup tomatoes, chopped
¼ cup spring onion whites, chopped
¼ cup spring onion greens, chopped
¼ cup cabbage, chopped
½ teaspoon lemon juice
¼ teaspoon red chilli powder
salt to taste

1. Soak the soyabeans in water for 2 to 3 hours. Drain and discard the water.
2. Add the turmeric and salt to the soyabeans, mix well and keep refrigerated
   overnight (6 to 8 hours).
3. Dry roast the soyabeans in a non-stick pan for 5 minutes, over medium heat,
   till they are partially crisp.
4. Mix the warm soyabeans with all the other ingredients and serve
   immediately.

*Handy tip : Cool the soyabeans and store in an air-tight container to have as a
dried snack.*

Nutritive values for per serving:

AMT	ENERGY	PROTEIN	CHO	FAT	FIBRE
gm	kcal	gm	gm	gm	gm
42	83	8.0	4.9	3.5	1.0

ACCOMPANIMENTS

 Carrot Garlic Chutney

Chutneys have always been the most favourite accompaniments with Indian dishes. This chutney is a mixture of carrot, to add fibre and garlic, to help maintain the required cholesterol levels and add that extra zing. This is a tasty accompaniment to the Sprouted Moong and Methi Chilas, page 41.

Preparation time : 30 minutes.   *No cooking.*   *Makes ½ cup. (approx. 7 tablespoons).*

1 cup carrots, thickly grated
2 tablespoons garlic, chopped
2 teaspoons chilli powder
¼ teaspoon lemon juice
1 teaspoon oil
1 teaspoon salt

1. Grind the garlic, chilli powder, lemon juice and salt to a fine paste in a blender.
2. Combine the carrots, garlic paste and oil in a bowl and mix well.
3. Store refrigerated in an air-tight container and use as required.

Nutritive values per tablespoon:

AMT	ENERGY	PROTEIN	CHO	FAT	FIBRE
gm	kcal	gm	gm	gm	gm
14	13	0.1	1.4	0.7	0.2

Garlic Tomato Salsa

Another lip smacking garlic delicacy, with loads of tomatoes to give the required texture to the salsa. This makes a good accompaniment to Crunchy Cumin Seed Crackers, page 61.

Preparation time : 10 minutes. *Cooking time : 15 minutes.* *Makes ¾ cup.*
(approx. 11 tablespoons).

6 to 8 large cloves garlic, finely chopped
¼ cup spring onion whites, chopped
1 tablespoon spring onion greens, finely chopped
2 dry red chilies, soaked
1 cup tomatoes, finely chopped
1 tablespoon finely chopped coriander
1 teaspoon olive oil or oil
salt to taste

1. Drain the soaked chillies and chop them finely.
2. Heat the oil, add the spring onion whites and garlic and sauté over a slow flame for 4 to 5 minutes till they are lightly brown.
3. Add the chillies and salt and sauté again.
4. Add the tomatoes and cook for 10 to 12 minutes over a slow flame till the tomatoes are soft and can be mashed lightly.
5. Cool completely and add the coriander and spring onion greens and mix well.
   Serve chilled or at room temperature.

Nutritive values per tablespoon:

AMT	ENERGY	PROTEIN	CHO	FAT	FIBRE
gm	kcal	gm	gm	gm	gm
18	9	0.2	0.9	0.5	0.1

Parsley Yoghurt Dip

Low fat yoghurt and spring onions team up with parsely to make this no fat dip which can be best relished with vegetable crudités or Soya Sesame Khakra, page 62. "Allicin" from garlic and the vitamin A and E from parsley together contribute to maintain the cholesterol levels in the blood, thus making this dip a nourishing accompaniment.

Preparation time : 15 minutes.   *No cooking.*   *Makes 1 cup.*
(approx. 14 tablespoons).

1 cup low fat curds (yoghurt), page 131
1 tablespoon finely chopped parsley
1 tablespoon spring onion greens, finely chopped
1½ teaspoons garlic, finely chopped
salt to taste

For serving
2 cups vegetable crudités (carrot, cucumber, radish, celery stalks)

1. Hang the curds in a muslin cloth for 15 to 20 minutes till it is thick.
2. Add all the other ingredients to this hung curd and blend in a liquidiser till it is smooth.
3. Serve chilled with vegetable crudités.

Handy tip : *Crudités are vegetables cut into French fries size.*

Nutritive values per tablespoon:

AMT	ENERGY	PROTEIN	CHO	FAT	FIBRE
gm	kcal	gm	gm	gm	gm
20	10	0.7	1.7	0.0	0.2

Herbed Hummus

Picture on page 111

Chick peas which are rich in protein, calcium and fibre are blended with vitamin A and E laden parsley to make this healthy dip. Enjoy it with whole wheat pita or simply use it as a sandwich spread to make a quick snack.

Preparation time : 5 minutes.   **No cooking.**   **Makes ¾ cup.**
(approx. 11 tablespoons).

½ cup chick peas (kabuli chana), boiled
½ cup parsley sprigs
2 tablespoons low fat curds, page 131
¼ teaspoon chopped garlic
¼ teaspoon lemon juice
1 teaspoon olive oil
salt to taste

Blend all the ingredients together in a blender till it is smooth.
Serve with whole wheat pita.

Nutritive values per tablespoon:

AMT	ENERGY	PROTEIN	CHO	FAT	FIBRE
gm	kcal	gm	gm	gm	gm
6	19	0.7	2.5	0.3	0.2

Chunky Vegetable Spread

Picture on page 86

This protein rich dip is low in fat yet filled with a wealth of flavours. Use it as a sandwich spread, to make an innovative filling as a substitute to calorie and fat laden cheese.

Preparation time : 15 minutes.   **No cooking.**   **Makes 1½ cups.**
(approx. 21 tablespoons).

2 tablespoons low fat milk, page 130
¾ cup low fat paneer (cottage cheese) page 132, grated

2 tablespoons chopped celery
¼ cup carrots, chopped
¼ cup capsicum, chopped
2 tablespoons chopped spring onion greens
2 tablespoons chopped tomatoes
¼ cup cucumber, chopped
1 tablespoon parsley, chopped
salt to taste

To serve
Crunchy Cumin Seed Crackers, page 61

1. Combine all ingredients in a bowl. Chill for 2 hours.
2. Serve with the crunchy cumin seed crackers.

Nutritive values per tablespoon:

AMT	ENERGY	PROTEIN	CHO	FAT	FIBRE
gm	kcal	gm	gm	gm	gm
10	13	1.3	1.9	0.0	0.1

 Coriander Garlic Chutney

This green chutney is a good way to help us consume garlic, especially as some of us are fussy about eating it raw. It gives best results when fresh garlic is in season. This chutney is absolutely low in calories and fat as it is devoid of fatty foods like peanuts and coconut. Instead these have been substituted with roasted Bengal gram dal.

Preparation time : 5 minutes.　　　　*No cooking.*　　　*Makes ½ cup.*
　　　　　　　　　　　　　　　　　　　　　　　　　(approx. 7 tablespoons).

½ cup fresh green garlic, chopped (including the greens)
1 cup coriander, finely chopped
1 teaspoon lemon juice
1 tablespoon roasted Bengal gram (daria)
½ cup water
salt to taste

Grind all the ingredients together in a blender to get a smooth chutney. Store refrigerated.

Nutritive values per tablespoon:

AMT	ENERGY	PROTEIN	CHO	FAT	FIBRE
gm	kcal	gm	gm	gm	gm
5	10	0.5	1.6	0.2	0.1

Handy tip : When fresh garlic is not in season, substitute it with 3 to 4 medium sized cloves of garlic.

 # High Fibre Chutney

Picture on page 25

The inclusion of this chutney may come as a surprise to some. The fibre in this chutney comes from green peas, which are added to the coriander. Garlic, lemon and as little as 1 teaspoon of sugar are added to perk up its flavours.

Preparation time : 5 minutes.   **No Cooking.**   **Makes 1 cup. (approx. 14 tablespoons).**

½ cup green peas, boiled
1 cup chopped coriander
1 to 2 green chillies
2 large cloves garlic
25 mm. (1") piece ginger
juice of ½ lemon
1 teaspoon sugar
salt to taste

1. Combine all the ingredients in a blender and grind to a fine paste using approx. 2 tablespoons water.
2. Refrigerate in an air-tight container.
3. Use as required.

Nutritive values per tablespoon:

AMT	ENERGY	PROTEIN	CHO	FAT	FIBRE
gm	kcal	gm	gm	gm	gm
7	7	0.4	1.3	0.0	0.2

Three Bean Salad

Picture on page 85

An excellent combination of mixed beans tossed in a tantalizing blend of herb dressing. The beans constitute a perfect low calorie way to add fibre to your diet.

Preparation time : 10 minutes.　　　*No cooking.*　　　*Serves 6.*

For the salad
3 cups mixed boiled beans (choose from rajma, chawli, chick peas, lima beans or hara chana)
½ cup spring onions, sliced
¾ cup tomatoes, diced

To be mixed into a dressing
1 teaspoon oil
2 tablespoons lemon juice
1 tablespoon chopped basil or ½ teaspoon dried oregano
½ teaspoon grated garlic
salt and pepper taste

For the garnish
2 tablespoons chopped coriander

1. Mix well all the ingredients together.
2. Add in the dressing and mix well. Refrigerate till required.
   Serve chilled garnished with the chopped coriander.

Nutritive values per serving:

AMT	ENERGY	PROTEIN	CHO	FAT	FIBRE
gm	kcal	gm	gm	gm	gm
77	156	8.9	25.7	2.3	2.1

Carrot and Mint Salad

Carrots combined with cucumber, kidney beans and spring onions are laced with a minty dressing. This salad, served with Lauki Kofta Curry, page 81, and Lachha Soya Paratha, page 98, make a completely yummy and healthy meal.

Preparation time : 10 minutes.　　　　*No cooking.*　　　　*Serves 2.*

1 cup carrots, peeled and thinly sliced
1 cup cucumber, peeled and thinly sliced
½ cup kidney beans (rajma), boiled
½ cup spring onions, sliced

To be mixed into a dressing
1 tablespoon finely chopped mint
1 teaspoon honey
1 tablespoon lemon juice
salt to taste

1. Combine all the ingredients for the salad in a bowl and chill.
2. Just before serving, add the dressing and toss well.
   Serve immediately.

Nutritive values per serving:

AMT	ENERGY	PROTEIN	CHO	FAT	FIBRE
gm	kcal	gm	gm	gm	gm
174	119	5.2	23.7	0.6	2.5

Bulgur Wheat Salad

This is a simple yet different way of adding a nutritious cereal like bulgur wheat to your meals. Being loaded with high fibre and nutrient dense veggies and dressed with a low fat curd dressing, this salad is, by all means, one of the best-suited salads for people with heart disease or high blood cholesterol levels.

Preparation time : 15 minutes.   **No cooking.**   **Serves 4.**

For the salad
½ cup bulgur wheat (dalia)
¼ cup carrots, finely chopped
¼ cup tomatoes, finely chopped
¼ cup capsicum, finely chopped
¼ cup mint, finely chopped
¼ cup spring onion greens, chopped
½ teaspoon lemon juice
salt to taste

To be mixed together into a dressing
½ cup low fat curds, page 131, whisked
¼ teaspoon garlic paste
salt to taste

1. Soak the bulgur wheat in hot water for 15 to 20 minutes. Drain and discard the water.
2. Mix together all the ingredients and refrigerate till required.
3. Add the dressing, toss lightly and serve immediately.

Nutritive values per serving:

AMT	ENERGY	PROTEIN	CHO .	FAT	FIBRE
gm	kcal	gm	gm	gm	gm
49	83	2.9	17.1	0.4	0.7

Lauki Phudina Raita

Picture on page 26

Raitas have always been a welcome addition to Indian meals. In this recipe, full fat curds have been replaced with low fat curds. The bottle gourd adds more body to this dish.

Preparation time : 5 minutes.   *Cooking time : 5 minutes.*   *Serves 3.*

1 cup bottle gourd (doodhi/lauki), grated
¼ tomato, chopped
1 cup low fat curds, page 131, whisked
2 tablespoons mint, chopped
¼ teaspoon roasted cumin seeds (jeera)
¼ teaspoon black salt (sanchal)
½ teaspoon sugar

1. Steam the bottle gourd for 4 to 5 minutes. Allow to cool completely.
2. Combine all the ingredients in a serving bowl and whisk well. Serve chilled.

Nutritive values per serving:

AMT	ENERGY	PROTEIN	CHO	FAT	FIBRE
gm	kcal	gm	gm	gm	gm
42	32	2.7	5.4	0.1	0.2

Cabbage, Carrot and Babycorn Stir-fry

Stir-fries are always on top of the list when it comes to healthy cooking to monitor the amount of fat used. Try this crunch filled combination of cabbage, carrot and baby corn.

Preparation time : 10 minutes.   *Cooking time : 10 minutes.*   *Serves 2.*

1 cup cabbage, sliced thinly

1 cup carrot, cut into thin strips
½ cup babycorn, sliced and parboiled
½ teaspoon cumin seeds (jeera)
1 green chilli, slit
1 teaspoon oil
salt to taste

1. Heat the oil and add the cumin seeds and green chilli.
2. When the cumin seeds crackle, add the cabbage, babycorn and carrots and salt and sauté over a medium flame for a few seconds.
3. Sprinkle a little water if required and continue to cook till it is soft. Serve at room temperature.

Nutritive values per serving:

AMT	ENERGY	PROTEIN	CHO	FAT	FIBRE
gm	kcal	gm	gm	gm	gm
136	94	2.4	16.2	2.7	1.9

Pear Salad

This unusual salad has its main ingredient as pear, which is also dressed with the pulp of the same fruit. Carrots and capsicum have been used in this salad, but you can make your own creation by adding other crispy vegetables like cabbage too. The lettuce can be replaced with any other leafy vegetable like radish leaves or salad leaves, to make these uncommon leafy vegetables a part of your diet.

Preparation time : 10 minutes.   *No cooking.*   *Serves 4.*

For the salad
¾ cup pears, chopped
¼ cup carrots, chopped
¼ cup capsicum, chopped
¼ cup bean sprouts
1 cup ice-berg lettuce, torn into small pieces

To be mixed together for the dressing
2 tablespoons pear pulp
½ teaspoon olive oil
¼ teaspoon prepared mustard paste
salt to taste

1. Mix all the ingredients for the salad together and chill.
2. Add the dressing and toss well.
    Serve immediately.

Nutritive values per serving:

AMT	ENERGY	PROTEIN	CHO	FAT	FIBRE
gm	kcal	gm	gm	gm	gm
92	48	2.0	8.0	0.9	0.8

 # Sweet Potato Salad

Combine the starchy sweet potato with other vegetables to add fibre to your diet. Another addition to this wonderful salad is walnuts, which helps to strengthen the heart and the apples lend the necessary sweetness while avoiding unnecessary calories from sugar.

Preparation time : 15 minutes.   *No cooking.*   *Serves 4.*

1 cup sweet potatoes, boiled and cut into 25 mm. (1") cubes
¾ cup apples, diced (unpeeled)
½ cup walnuts, chopped
½ cup celery, chopped
½ cup capsicum, cut into 25 mm. (1") cubes
1 teaspoon lemon juice

To be mixed together for the dressing
½ cup low fat curds, page 131
½ teaspoon prepared mustard paste
salt and pepper to taste

1. Mix all the ingredients together in a large bowl an refrigerate. Serve chilled.

AMT	ENERGY	PROTEIN	CHO	FAT	FIBRE
gm	kcal	gm	gm	gm	gm
108	175	3.4	16.3	10.8	1.3

 # *Italian Style Tossed Salad*

This salad is a healthy mixture of a selection of low cal veggies, which can be put together in no time at all. The olive oil and basil dressing lends this salad an exotic flavour.

Preparation time : 10 minutes.   **No cooking.**   **Serves 4.**

2 cups ice-berg lettuce, torn into small pieces
½ cup mushrooms, sliced and blanched
½ cup broccoli florets, boiled
½ cup carrots, diced and boiled
¼ cup onions, cut into 25 mm. (1") cubes

To be mixed into a dressing
1 teaspoon honey
1 teaspoon lemon juice
1 tablespoon chopped basil
salt and freshly crushed pepper to taste

1. Combine all the ingredients together and refrigerate till required.
2. Toss the salad with the dressing and serve immediately.

Nutritive values per serving:

AMT	ENERGY	PROTEIN	CHO	FAT	FIBRE
gm	kcal	gm	gm	gm	gm
112	36	2.4	6.2	0.8	0.8

Soya Vegetable Korma

Picture on cover

Soya nuggets, a variation of soyabeans, have been used in this recipe and cooked in a white gravy. The traditional use of cashews in this recipe has been substituted with cauliflower purée, making this a healthy gravy.

Preparation time : 15 minutes.   *Cooking time : 20 minutes.*   *Serves 4.*

¼ cup small soya nuggets
1 cup mixed vegetables (French beans, peas, carrots), diced and boiled
½ cup onions, chopped
1 teaspoon ginger-green chilli paste
½ cup tomatoes, chopped
½ cup fenugreek (methi) leaves, chopped
1 teaspoon oil
salt to taste

For the paste
1¼ cups onions, sliced
¼ cup cauliflower, finely chopped
1 to 2 green chillies, chopped
2 large cloves garlic, chopped
12 mm. (½") piece ginger, sliced
1 stick cinnamon (dalchini)
1 clove (laung)
1 cup low fat milk, page 130

For the paste
1. Combine all the ingredients in a pan and simmer for 8 to 10 minutes till the onions are soft and nearly all the liquid has evaporated. Allow the mixture to cool.
2. Purée the mixture to a smooth paste in a blender. Keep aside.

How to proceed
1. Soak the soya nuggets in hot water for 10 to 15 minutes. Drain all the water and squeeze out any excess water from the nuggets.
2. Heat the oil, add the onions, ginger-green chilli paste and cook till the onions turn translucent.

3. Add the tomatoes, fenugreek leaves and cook for 5 to 6 minutes till the tomatoes are cooked.
4. Add the vegetables, soya nuggets, the prepared paste, ½ cup water and salt and bring the mixture to a boil.
Serve hot.

Nutritive values per serving:

AMT	ENERGY	PROTEIN	CHO	FAT	FIBRE
gm	kcal	gm	gm	gm	gm
109	113	8.0	12.7	3.3	1.5

Lauki Kofta Curry

These koftas are prepared with lauki in a larger proportion, in comparison to potato, to minimize the caloric value of the dish. Also, koftas are not deep fried, but are simmered and cooked in the gravy itself. This makes a tasty combination with Lachha Soya Paratha, page 98.

Preparation time : 15 minutes.   *Cooking time : 20 minutes.*   *Serves 4.*

For the lauki koftas
1½ cups bottle gourd (doodhi / lauki), grated
½ cup Bengal gram flour (besan)
⅓ cup potato, boiled and mashed
1 teaspoon ginger and garlic paste
1 to 2 green chillies, chopped
1 teaspoon chaat masala
salt to taste

For the gravy
1 teaspoon cumin seeds (jeera)
½ cup onions, grated
1 teaspoon ginger paste
1 teaspoon garlic paste
½ cup tomatoes, grated

½ teaspoon turmeric powder (haldi)
½ teaspoon coriander-cumin seed (dhania-jeera) powder
½ teaspoon chilli powder
½ teaspoon garam masala
½ teaspoon corn flour
2 to 3 tablespoons low fat milk, page 130
1 teaspoon oil
salt to taste

For the lauki koftas

1. Strain the juice out of the grated bottlegourd and preserve it to add in the gravy.
2. Combine all the ingredients together and transfer it into a non-stick pan and stir it over medium heat till the mixture leaves the sides of the pan.
3. Remove and cool slightly. Divide this mixture into 12 to 16 equal portions and roll into koftas. Keep aside.

For the gravy

1. Heat the oil in a pan and add the cumin seeds.
2. When they crackle, add the onions and sauté for 2 to 3 minutes.
3. Add the ginger paste, garlic paste and sauté for 1 more minute.
4. Add the grated tomatoes, turmeric powder, coriander-cumin seed powder and chilli powder and cook till the oil separates from the masala.
5. Dissolve the cornflour in milk and keep aside.
6. Add 2 cups of water to the gravy and bring to a boil (you can add the bottle gourd juice too).
7. Add the koftas and the milk and cornflour mixture and simmer for 4 to 5 minutes.
8. Sprinkle the garam masala and bring to a boil.
   Serve hot.

Handy tip : The koftas tend to crumble if you boil them too much in the gravy. So, its better to add them just before you're ready to serve them.

Nutritive values per serving:

AMT	ENERGY	PROTEIN	CHO	FAT	FIBRE
gm	kcal	gm	gm	gm	gm
113	85	3.1	13.6	2.0	0.8

Paneer Lababdar

Low fat paneer cubes in an aromatic, spicy gravy with sautéed onions, this vegetable is sure to be the talk of your meal. Ensure that the paneer has maintained its softness, though. To master the art of making low fat paneer in your own kitchen refer to page 132. This subzi makes a perfect combination with Oat and Spring Onion Paratha, page 97.

Preparation time : 10 minutes.　　　*Cooking time : 15 minutes.*　　　*Serves 4.*

1 cup low fat paneer (cottage cheese), page 132, cut into cubes
½ teaspoon cumin seeds (jeera)
1 teaspoon coriander (dhania) seeds, roasted and crushed
3 whole red chillies, coarsely ground
½ teaspoon dried fenugreek (kasuri methi leaves)
½ cup onions, finely chopped
1½ teaspoons ginger-garlic paste
¼ teaspoon turmeric powder (haldi)
1½ cups tomatoes, chopped
½ cup low fat milk, page 131
¼ teaspoon cornflour
¼ teaspoon garam masala
1 teaspoon oil
salt to taste

For the garnish
2 tablespoons chopped coriander

1. Heat the oil in a non-stick pan, add the cumin seeds, coriander seeds, ground chillies, dried fenugreek leaves and onions and sauté till the onions turn light brown in colour.
2. Add the ginger-garlic paste, turmeric powder, tomatoes with 4 tablespoons of water and cook till the oil separates from the masala.
3. Cool the masala mixture and purée to a smooth paste and transfer into a non-stick pan.
4. Dissolve the cornflour in the milk and add it to the prepared gravy and simmer for 3 to 4 minutes.
5. Add the paneer, garam masala and salt and mix well.
    Serve hot garnished with the chopped coriander.

AMT	ENERGY	PROTEIN	CHO	FAT	FIBRE
gm	kcal	gm	gm	gm	gm
102	118	9.9	16.3	1.4	0.6

Palak Kadhi

This is an unusual way of adding nurients by way of greens to your meal. Serve hot with steamed rice and a big bowl of salad to end your lunch.

Preparation time : 10 minutes.　　　*Cooking time : 15 minutes.*　　　*Serves 4.*

1 cup low fat curds, page 131, whisked
2 tablespoons Bengal gram flour (besan)
1 cup spinach (palak), chopped
1 teaspoon cumin seeds (jeera)
¼ cup onions, chopped
1 teaspoon ginger-chilli paste
a pinch turmeric powder (haldi)
¼ teaspoon chilli powder
a pinch sugar (optional)
2 teaspoons oil
salt to taste

1. In a bowl, add the curds, gram flour and 1 cup of water and whisk till the mixture is smooth. Keep aside
2. Heat the oil in a non-stick pan, and add the cumin seeds.
3. When the seeds crackle, add the onions, ginger-chilli paste, turmeric powder and chilli powder and sauté for 2 to 3 minutes.
4. Add the curds mixture, salt and sugar and allow it to come to a boil, while stirring continuously.
5. Add the spinach and serve hot with steamed rice and a bowl of salad.

Nutritive values per serving:

AMT	ENERGY	PROTEIN	CHO	FAT	FIBRE
gm	kcal	gm	gm	gm	gm
36	59	3.2	6.6	2.2	0.5

Chana Palak

Chick peas cooked in a different mild gravy made with spinach purée and tomato. Skim milk powder has been added for thickening, giving a velvety texture without any fat component.

Preparation time : 15 minutes.   *Cooking time : 15 minutes.*   *Serves 2.*

5 cups spinach (palak), chopped
½ cup boiled chick peas (kabuli chana)
1 teaspoon cumin seeds (jeera)
½ cup onions, chopped
½ teaspoon garlic, chopped
1 teaspoon ginger-green chilli paste
¼ cup tomatoes, chopped
1 teaspoon skim milk powder
1 teaspoon oil
salt to taste

1. Blanch the spinach in hot water for a few seconds.
2. Transfer it into cold water and drain.
3. Purée the spinach to a paste and keep aside.
4. Heat the oil in a non-stick pan, add the cumin seeds and allow them to crackle.
5. Add the onions, garlic, ginger-green chilli paste and cook till the onions turn golden brown in colour, adding a little water to moisten if the onions burn.
6. Add the spinach purée, tomatoes and milk powder along with the ½ cup of water and cook for 3 minutes.
7. Add the chick peas and salt and simmer for another 2 minutes.
   Serve hot with parathas.

Nutritive values per serving:

AMT	ENERGY	PROTEIN	CHO	FAT	FIBRE
gm	kcal	gm	gm	gm	gm
249	172	8.6	23.3	4.9	2.2

Pyazwali Bhindi

A perfect low calorie version of the famous North-Indian delicacy in which the ladies finger is tossed with sautéed onions. Traditionally the bhindis are deep-fried to whip up this delicacy. Here is a heart-friendly variation to enjoy your favourite subzi and yet keep a check on calories as well as fat.

Preparation time : 15 minutes.   *Cooking time : 15 minutes.*   *Serves 2.*

2 cups ladies finger, chopped
1 teaspoon cumin seeds (jeera)
1 cup onions, chopped
2 teaspoons ginger-green chilli paste
a pinch turmeric powder (haldi)
¼ cup low fat curds, page 131
2 teaspoons oil
salt to taste

1. Heat the oil in a non-stick pan, add the cumin seeds and allow them to crackle.
2. Add the onions, ginger-green chilli paste, turmeric powder and cook till the onions turn golden brown.
3. Add the bhindi and cook over medium flame till they are soft.
4. Add the curds and salt and cook for 2 to 3 more minutes.
   Serve hot with parathas.

Nutritive values per serving:

AMT	ENERGY	PROTEIN	CHO	FAT	FIBRE
gm	kcal	gm	gm	gm	gm
146	120	4.0	14.4	5.2	1.2

Gavarfali with Bajra Dhokli

Gavarfali and bajra, the two fibre rich ingredients have been combined to make this mouth-watering delicacy. Served hot with phulkas to make a hearty and healthy meal.

Preparation time : a few minutes.　　　*Cooking time : 25 minutes.*　　　*Serves 4.*

2 cups gavarfali (cluster beans), cut into 25 mm. (1") pieces
½ teaspoon cumin seeds (jeera)
½ teaspoon ajwain (carom seeds)
1 teaspoon ginger-green chilli paste
¼ teaspoon turmeric powder (haldi)
½ teaspoon sugar
salt to taste
1 teaspoon oil

For the bajra dhokli
½ cup bajra flour (black millet flour)
1 tablespoon whole wheat flour (gehun ka atta)
½ teaspoon garlic, finely chopped
1 tablespoon chopped coriander
1 teaspoon oil
salt to taste

For the bajra dhokli
1. Combine all the ingredients together and mix well.
2. Add a little warm water and knead into firm dough.
3. Divide into 20 equal portions and shape them into rounds.
4. Press each portion into a flat circle by pressing between your palms. Keep aside.

How to proceed
1. Heat the oil and add the cumin seeds and ajwain.
2. When they crackle, add the gavarfali and salt and sauté for a few minutes.
3. Add 3 cups of water, ginger-green chilli paste, turmeric powder and simmer for 10 to 12 minutes till the gavarfali is soft.
4. Add the dhoklis into the simmering vegetable and simmer for 5 to 7 minutes till the dhoklis are cooked. Add ½ cup of warm water if required to adjust the consistency.
Serve hot.

Nutritive values per serving:

AMT	ENERGY	PROTEIN	CHO	FAT	FIBRE
gm	kcal	gm	gm	gm	gm
68	84	3.3	15.7	3.3	1.8

DALS

Panch Ratani Dal

This is a delightful combination of dals simmered with aromatic spices that lend to bouquet of tantalizing flavours, along with all the nutrients that dals add to our diet.

Preparation time : 15 minutes.   *Cooking time : 25 minutes.*   *Serves 6.*

¼ cup whole moong (whole green gram)
¼ cup whole masoor (whole red lentils)
¼ cup urad (whole black lentils)
¼ cup chana dal (split Bengal gram)
¼ cup toovar (arhar) dal
3 cardamoms (elaichi)
25 mm. (1") stick cinnamon (dalchini)
1 teaspoon cumin seeds (jeera)
½ cup onions, chopped
¼ cup tomatoes, chopped
1 teaspoon coriander (dhania) powder
2 teaspoons chilli powder
¼ teaspoon turmeric powder (haldi)
½ teaspoon cumin seed (jeera) powder
1½ teaspoons fennel (saunf) powder
½ cup low fat curds, page 131, whisked
2 teaspoons oil

For the garnish
2 tablespoons chopped coriander

1. Wash and soak the dals in warm water for at least an hour. Drain and keep aside.
2. Add 4 cups water and cook in a pressure cooker for 15 to 20 minutes, over medium flame, till the dals are cooked.
3. Heat the oil in a pan, add the cardamoms, cinnamon and cumin seeds and allow the cumin seeds to crackle.
4. Add the onions and cook till they are golden brown.
5. Add the tomatoes, coriander powder, red chilli powder, turmeric powder, cumin seed powder and fennel powder and cook for 4 to 5 minutes.

6. Add the curds and cook for 2 to 3 minutes.
7. Add the cooked dals and salt and allow the dal to come to a boil.
8. Garnish with coriander and serve hot with rice or rotis.

Nutritive values per serving:

AMT	ENERGY	PROTEIN	CHO	FAT	FIBRE
gm	kcal	gm	gm	gm	gm
56	143	8.8	22.5	2.0	0.7

Dhabey Ki Dal

A pan of mixed pulses, seasoned with spices and lots of garlic, cooked in just 2 teaspoons of oil. This dal tastes best with a bowl of rice, followed by a high fibre fruit like guava or orange, to end the meal.

Preparation time : 15 minutes.   *Cooking time : 30 minutes.*   *Serves 4.*

½ cup urad dal (split black lentils), with skin
¼ cup chana dal (split Bengal gram)
¼ cup red kidney beans (rajma)
1 cup onions, finely chopped
1 tablespoon garlic, finely chopped
2 green chillies, slit into 2
1 cup tomato, finely chopped
1 teaspoon chilli powder
2 teaspoons cumin (jeera) powder
¼ cup fresh coriander leaves, chopped
1 tablespoon kasuri methi (dried fenugreek leaves)
2 teaspoons oil
salt to taste

1. Clean, wash and soak the urad dal, chana dal and kidney beans in sufficient water for at least 6 hours.
2. Drain the soaked dals, add six cups water and pressure cook for 15 to 20 minutes or unitl the dals completely cooked.
3. Heat the oil in a non-stick pan, add the garlic, onions and green chillies and sauté for 4 to 5 minutes till the onions are golden brown in colour.

4. Add the tomatoes, chilli powder, cumin powder and salt and cook over a high flame for 3 to 4 minutes.
5. Add the cooked dals and coriander, mix well and simmer for 5 to 7 minutes.
6. Add the kasuri methi, mix well and serve hot.

Nutritive values per serving:

AMT	ENERGY	PROTEIN	CHO	FAT	FIBRE
gm	kcal	gm	gm	gm	gm
104	140	7.4	22.7	2.2	1.2

 Chana Dal with Cucumber

Chana dal in addition to protein provides a good source of iron and fibre while cucumber, added to enhance the flavours, contributes minimal calories and no fat to your diet. Serve hot with rice or chapatis to square up your meal.

Preparation time : 10 minutes.   *Cooking time : 20 minutes.*   *Serves 4.*

¾ cup chana dal (split Bengal gram)
½ cup cucumber, finely chopped
1 teaspoon cumin seeds (jeera)
1 teaspoon ginger-green chilli paste
a pinch turmeric powder (haldi)
½ teaspoon chilli powder
1 teaspoon oil
salt to taste

For the garnish
1 tablespoon chopped coriander

1. Wash and soak the chana dal in water for at least an hour. Drain and keep aside.
2. Add 2 cups water to the soaked dal and pressure cook for 10 to 15 minutes, till the dal is cooked.

3. Heat the oil in a non-stick pan, add the cumin seeds and allow them to crackle.
4. Add the cooked dal, ginger-green chilli paste, turmeric powder and chilli powder and cook for 2 to 3 minutes.
5. Add the cucumber and salt and simmer for 10 to 15 minutes till the cucumber is tender, but still a little crisp. Add some water, if required to adjust the consistency.
6. Garnish with the coriander and serve hot with rice or chapatis.

Nutritive values per serving:

AMT	ENERGY	PROTEIN	CHO	FAT	FIBRE
gm	kcal	gm	gm	gm	gm
48	124	5.3	19.2	2.9	1.3

 # Palak Masoor Dal

A fragrant spinach and lentil preparation made without the use of any calorie-laden ingredients. Enjoy this dal with phulkas or parathas made on a non-stick pan by only brushing the parathas with oil and not adding extra oil to cook them. Do remember not to overcook this dal as the spinach tends to discolour.

Preparation time : 10 minutes.   **Cooking time : 20 minutes.**   *Serves 4.*

½ cup masoor dal (split red lentils)
1 cup spinach (palak), chopped
1 teaspoon ginger-green chilli paste
a pinch turmeric powder (haldi)
1 tablespoon tamarind (imli) pulp
salt to taste

For the tempering
3 cardamoms (elaichi)
1 teaspoon cumin seeds (jeera)
3 dry red chillies, broken
6 to 8 curry leaves
1 teaspoon garlic, chopped
1 teaspoon oil

1. Wash and soak the masoor dal in water for an hour. Drain and discard the water.
2. Add the ginger-green chilli paste and turmeric to the dal alongwith 2 cups of water and pressure cook for 10 to 15 minutes, until the dal is cooked.

For the tempering
1. Heat the oil in a pan, add the cardamoms and cumin seeds and allow them to crackle.
2. Add the dry red chillies, curry leaves and garlic and sauté for 1 minute.

How to proceed
Pour the tempering over the cooked dal, add the tamarind pulp, spinach and salt and allow the dal to come to a boil. Simmer for a few minutes and serve hot.

Nutritive values per serving:

AMT	ENERGY	PROTEIN	CHO	FAT	FIBRE
gm	kcal	gm	gm	gm	gm
39	85	5.4	12.5	1.5	0.3

Methiwali Dal

This dal serves a dual purpose—it's extremely good for people with heart ailments along with diabetes as methi helps to control blood sugar levels. I have added ginger and garlic to this dal which gives the perfect spice effect and helps to avoid the need of oil-laden pickles. Serve hot with Stuffed Soya Parathas, page 100.

Preparation time : 10 minutes.   *Cooking time : 20 minutes.*   *Serves 4.*

1 cup toovar (arhar) dal
½ cup fenugreek (methi) leaves, chopped
1 teaspoon cumin seeds (jeera)
¼ cup onions, chopped
1 teaspoon chopped garlic
2 teaspoons chopped ginger

1 teaspoon green chillies, chopped
¼ cup tomatoes, chopped
½ teaspoon chilli powder
a pinch turmeric powder (haldi)
1 teaspoon lemon juice
1 teaspoon oil
salt to taste

1. Wash and soak the dal in water for an hour. Drain and discard the water. Add 2 cups water and cook in a pressure cooker for 10 to 15 minutes till the dal is cooked.
2. Heat the oil in a non-stick pan, add the cumin seeds and allow them to crackle.
3. Add the onions, garlic, ginger and green chillies and cook till the onions are translucent.
4. Add the fenugreek leaves and sauté over high flame for 1 minute.
5. Add the tomatoes, chilli powder and turmeric powder and cook for 2 to 3 minutes.
6. Add the cooked dal and salt and allow the dal to come a boil. Simmer for 4 to 5 minutes.
7. Add the lemon juice, mix well and serve hot.

Nutritive values per serving:

AMT	ENERGY	PROTEIN	CHO	FAT	FIBRE
gm	kcal	gm	gm	gm	gm
70	160	9.7	25.6	2.1	0.9

Oat and Spring Onion Parathas

Picture on cover.

These paratha are made with a combination of oats and wheat flour to initiate you to the taste of fibre filled oats. I have used the spring onion filling as it helps to disguise the raw taste of oats. This serves best when served hot with Paneer Lababdar, page 83.

Preparation time : 15 minutes.   **Cooking time : 20 minutes.**   **Makes 4 parathas.**

For the dough
¾ cup whole wheat flour (gehun ka atta)
¼ cup quick cooking rolled oats
2 tablespoons low fat curds, page 131
salt to taste

For the spring onion filling
½ cup spring onion whites, chopped
1 cup spring onion greens, chopped
1 teaspoon cumin seeds (jeera)
1 teaspoon ginger-green chilli paste
1 teaspoon garlic, finely chopped
½ teaspoon oil
salt to taste

Other ingredients
1 teaspoon oil for cooking

For the dough
1. Combine all the ingredients and knead into a soft dough, using enough water.
2. Divide into 4 equal portions and keep aside.

For the spring onion filling
1. Heat the oil in a non-stick pan, add the cumin seeds and allow them to crackle.
2. Add the spring onion whites, ginger-green chilli paste, garlic and cook till the onions turn translucent.

3. Add the spring onion greens and salt and cook over a high flame till the mixture dries out completely. Remove and let it cool.

How to proceed
1. Roll out the one portion of the dough into a circle of 75 mm. (3") diameter.
2. Place one portion of the filling in the centre of the dough circle.
3. Bring together all the sides in the centre and seal tightly.
4. Roll out again into a circle of 125 mm. (5") diameter with the help of a little plain flour.
5. Cook the paratha on a non-stick pan, using a little oil, until both sides are golden brown.
6. Repeat with the remaining dough and filling to make 3 more paratha. Serve hot.

Nutritive values per paratha:

AMT	ENERGY	PROTEIN	CHO	FAT	FIBRE
gm	kcal	gm	gm	gm	gm
52	117	3.9	19.8	2.6	1.1

 Lachha Soya Paratha

A simple yet mouth-watering delicacy made by combining 2 fibre laden ingredients whole wheat flour and soya flour, to keep a check on your blood cholestero levels. Try out one paratha and you are sure to be tempted to go for a second one.

Preparation time : 30 minutes.   *Cooking time : 30 minutes.*   *Makes 6 parathas.*

½ cups wheat flour (gehun ka atta)
¼ cup soya flour
salt to taste

Other ingredients
¼ cup coriander, chopped
1 teaspoon chilli powder
1 teaspoon roasted cumin (jeera) powder

½ teaspoon salt
1 teaspoon oil for cooking

1. Combine the wheat flour, soya flour and salt and knead into a semi-soft dough using enough water. Keep aside for 10 to 15 minutes.
2. Combine the coriander, chilli powder, cumin powder and salt in a dry bowl and mix well.
3. Divide the dough into 6 equal parts.
4. Roll out each portion into a large chapati about 125 mm. (5") in diameter.
5. Place one rolled chapati on to a clean dry surface and sprinkle some of the coriander mixture evenly on the surface.
6. Top with one more chapati and sprinkle some of the coriander mixture.
7. Repeat to complete the remaining 4 chapatis by piling them on top of each other.
8. Press them down firmly and then roll them together like a Swiss roll, sealing the edges by pinching them.
9. Cut the roll vertically into 6 equal parts.
10. Place one portion on marble top and roll into a circle about 125 mm. (5") in diameter.
11. Cook on a non-stick pan over medium flame till the paratha is golden brown on both the sides.
12. Combine the oil with 1 teaspoon of water in a bowl and use this to grease the paratha lightly.
13. Repeat to make the remaining 5 parathas.
Serve immediately to avoid the parathas turning soggy.

Nutritive values per paratha:

AMT	ENERGY	PROTEIN	CHO	FAT	FIBRE
gm	kcal	gm	gm	gm	gm
32	112	4.5	19.4	1.9	0.6

Stuffed Soya Paratha

Green peas, stuffed in wheat flour dough to make parathas, is very common. In this recipe, soya and garlic have been added to the wheat flour, to make it extremely 'heart-friendly'. Serve them hot from the tava, as soya tends to make the parathas dry after a while, especially as these are made with minimal oil.

Preparation time : 15 minutes.   Cooking time : 30 minutes.   Makes 6 parathas.

For the dough
1 cup whole wheat flour (gehun ka atta)
½ cup soya flour
1 teaspoon garlic, grated
salt to taste

For the filling
1 cup green peas, boiled and mashed
1 teaspoon cumin seeds (jeera)
1 teaspoon ginger-green chilli paste
1 teaspoon chilli powder
1 teaspoon coriander (dhania) powder
½ teaspoon cumin (jeera) powder .
½ teaspoon amchur (dry mango powder)
a pinch turmeric powder (haldi)
1 teaspoon oil
salt to taste

Other ingredients
1 teaspoon oil for cooking

For the dough
1. Combine all the ingredients together to make a semi-soft dough using enough water.
2. Divide into 6 equal portions and keep aside.

For the filling
1. Heat the oil in a non-stick pan, add the cumin seeds and allow the seeds to crackle.

2. Add the remaining ingredients and cook for 3 to 4 minutes.
3. Remove and allow to cool.

How to proceed

1. Roll out one portion of the dough into a circle of 75 mm. (3") diameter.
2. Place one portion of the filling in the center of the dough circle.
3. Bring together all the sides in the center and seal tightly.
4. Roll out again into a circle of 125 mm. (5") diameter with the help of a little flour.
5. Cook the paratha on a non-stick pan, using a little oil until both sides are golden brown.
6. Repeat with the remaining dough and filling to make 5 more parathas. Serve hot.

Nutritive values per paratha:

AMT	ENERGY	PROTEIN	CHO	FAT	FIBRE
gm	kcal	gm	gm	gm	gm
49	123	6.3	17.4	3.1	1.5

Pyaz ki Roti

A simple preparation with the addition of wheat bran to wheat flour, to enhance your fibre intake. Initially start with 2 tablespoons of bran and once you have adapted to it, feel free to double the quantity of wheat bran.

Preparation time : 10 minutes.   **Cooking time : 15 minutes.**   **Makes 4 rotis.**

1 cup whole wheat flour (gehun ka atta)
2 tablespoons wheat bran
3 teaspoons anardana (dried pomegranate seeds), roasted and powdered
½ cup onions, finely chopped
1 teaspoon green chillies, finely chopped
1 teaspoon oil
salt to taste

Other ingredients

1 teaspoon oil for cooking

1. Mix together all the ingredients and knead into a soft dough adding enough water.
2. Divide the dough into 4 equal portions and roll out to a circle of 125 mm. (5") diameter.
3. Cook on a non-stick pan till both sides are lightly browned, using a little oil.
4. Repeat to make 3 more rotis.
   Serve hot with a subzi of your choice.

Nutritive values per roti:

AMT	ENERGY	PROTEIN	CHO	FAT	FIBRE
gm	kcal	gm	gm	gm	gm
52	144	4.4	24.3	3.3	1.2

 ## *Bajra aur Kaddu ki Roti*

A full meal in itself, this dish is best for days when you don't have the time to cook, or have unexpected guests. Just serve the rotis with a bowl of low fat curds and salad and your meal is done.

Preparation time : 10 minutes.   *Cooking time : 10 minutes.*   *Makes 6 rotis.*

½ cup bajra flour (black millet flour)
½ cup whole wheat flour (gehun ka atta)
1 cup pumpkin (kaddu), grated
1 teaspoon ginger-green chilli paste
a pinch turmeric powder (haldi)
¼ teaspoon asafoetida (hing)
1 teaspoon lemon juice
2 tablespoons chopped coriander
salt to taste

Other ingredients

1 teaspoon oil for cooking

1. Mix all the ingredients together, except the oil and make a semi-soft dough using enough water. Keep covered for 10 to 15 minutes.
2. Divide the dough into 6 equal portions and shape into round balls.
3. Roll out each portion into 125 mm. (5") diameter rounds.
4. Cook on a non-stick pan, using a little oil, till both sides are lightly browned.
5. Repeat to make 5 more rotis.
   Serve hot.

Nutritive values per roti:

AMT	ENERGY	PROTEIN	CHO	FAT	FIBRE
gm	kcal	gm	gm	gm	gm
42	74	2.4	12.9	1.4	0.5

Tava Sprouts Pulao

Picture on page 26

Mildly spiced rice, to which sprouts and veggies have been added, is garnished with mint, to enhance its flavours.

Sprouting pulses leads to the production of enzyme called "amylase" which helps in enhancing the process of digestion. The pulses when combined with any other cereal like rice, as I have done in this recipe, are a better source of protein than when consumed on their own.

Preparation time : 20 minutes.   *Cooking time : 15 minutes.*   *Serves 4.*

1½ cups boiled rice
½ cup moong (whole green gram) sprouts, boiled
½ cup matki (moath beans) sprouts, boiled
1 teaspoon cumin seeds (jeera)
½ cup onions, chopped
1 cup tomatoes, chopped
1 teaspoon ginger, finely chopped
1 teaspoon garlic, finely chopped
½ cup capsicum, chopped
½ teaspoon chilli powder
a pinch turmeric powder (haldi)
1 teaspoon pav bhaji masala (optional)
1 teaspoon oil
salt to taste

For the garnish
2 tablespoons chopped mint

1. Heat the oil in a non-stick pan, add the cumin seeds and allow them to crackle.
2. Add the onions and cook till they turn translucent.
3. Add the tomatoes, ginger, garlic, capsicum, chilli powder, turmeric powder and pav bhaji masala and cook till the oil separates from the mixture.
4. Add the moong sprouts, matki sprouts, rice and salt. Mix well and cook for 3 to 4 minutes.
    Serve hot garnished with the chopped mint.

AMT	ENERGY	PROTEIN	CHO	FAT	FIBRE
gm	kcal	gm	gm	gm	gm
109	149	5.7	27.9	1.7	1.3

Whole Wheat and Vegetable Khichdi

This dish is most suited to people having diabetes and high cholesterol, as rice has been replaced with whole wheat. This khichdi, spiced with a mixture of Indian spices, tastes best when served hot with a bowl of curds and Carrot Garlic Chutney, page 66.

Preparation time : 15 minutes.   **Cooking time : 15 minutes.**   **Serves 4.**
Soaking time : 6 to 8 hours.

½ cup whole wheat (gehun)
½ cup moong dal (split green gram), soaked for 15 to 20 minutes
1 cup mixed vegetables (carrot, cauliflower, French beans, peas), diced
3 peppercorns
3 cloves (laung)
25 mm. (1") stick cinnamon (dalchini)
1 bay leaf (tejpatta)
1 teaspoon cumin seeds (jeera)
a pinch asafoetida (hing)
¼ cup onions, sliced
2 teaspoons chilli powder
1 teaspoon cumin (jeera) powder
2 teaspoons coriander (dhania) powder
a pinch turmeric powder (haldi)
1 teaspoon oil
salt to taste

1. Wash and soak the whole wheat for 6 to 8 hours. Drain and discard the water.
2. Grind the whole wheat in a mixer to a coarse paste adding approx. ½ cup water. Keep aside.
3. Heat the oil in a pressure cooker, add the peppercorns, cloves, cinnamon, bay leaf and cumin seeds and allow the cumin seeds to crackle.

4. Add the asafoetida, onions and cook till the onions turn translucent.
5. Add the vegetables and sauté for 2 to 3 minutes.
6. Add the ground wheat, moong dal, chilli powder, cumin powder, coriander powder, turmeric powder and salt and mix well.
7. Add 3½ cups water, mix well and allow the water to come to a boil.
8. Pressure cook the khichdi over a medium flame for 10 minutes. Serve hot.

Nutritive values per serving:

AMT	ENERGY	PROTEIN	CHO	FAT	FIBRE
gm	kcal	gm	gm	gm	gm
70	169	8.3	29.6	1.9	1.2

Cabbage Pulao

This is an easy to make rice delicacy, put together especially for South Indian food fans. This recipe makes use of cabbage and a tempering of urad dal, both ingredients being most popular in South Indian cooking.

Preparation time : 10 minutes.　　　*Cooking time : 10 minutes.*　　　*Serves 2.*

1 cup boiled rice
1 cup cabbage, shredded
½ teaspoon mustard seeds (rai)
½ teaspoon urad dal (split black lentils)
a pinch asafoetida (hing)
4 to 5 curry leaves
3 dry red chillies, broken into 25 mm. (1") pieces
¼ cup onions, thinly sliced
a pinch turmeric powder (haldi)
½ teaspoon lemon juice
¼ cup chana dal (split Bengal gram), parboiled
1 teaspoon oil
salt to taste

For the garnish
1 tablespoon chopped coriander

1. Heat the oil in a non-stick pan, add the mustard seeds and allow them to crackle.
2. Add the urad dal, asafoetida, curry leaves and dry red chillies and cook for 1 minute till the urad dal turns pink.
3. Add the onions and turmeric powder and cook for another minute.
4. Add the cabbage, chana dal, salt and 1 tablespoon water and cook over a low flame for 5 minutes or till the cabbage is tender.
5. Add the rice and lemon juice, mix well and cook covered for a few minutes. Serve hot garnished with the chopped coriander.

Nutritive values per serving:

AMT	ENERGY	PROTEIN	CHO	FAT	FIBRE
gm	kcal	gm	gm	gm	gm
102	157	6.1	29.4	3.9	0.8

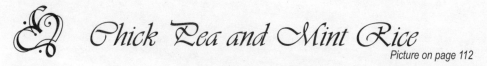

Chick Pea and Mint Rice
Picture on page 112

An all-in-one satiating delicacy made with ingredients from 4 food groups—cereals (rice), pulses (chick peas), vegetables and oil. All it needs is a calcium rich bowl of low fat curds to make a complete meal.

Preparation time : 15 minutes.   *Cooking time : 15 to 20 minutes.*   *Serves 4.*

1 cup rice, washed and soaked
½ cup boiled chick peas (kabuli chana),
½ cup mixed vegetables (French beans, carrots, peas), chopped
½ cup onions, sliced
½ teaspoon garlic, chopped
1 bay leaf (tejpatta)
¼ cup mint, chopped
½ teaspoon lemon juice
1 teaspoon oil
salt to taste

1. Heat the oil in a non-stick pan, add the onions, garlic and bay leaf and cook till the onions are soft.
2. Add the vegetables, rice, 2 cups water and salt and cook over medium flame till the rice is partially cooked.
3. Add the chick peas, mint and lemon juice, mix well and cook covered over low flame till the rice is cooked.
   Serve hot.

Nutritive values per serving:

AMT	ENERGY	PROTEIN	CHO	FAT	FIBRE
gm	kcal	gm	gm	gm	gm
90	199	5.1	39.9	2.1	0.9

Baked Vegetable Roll Up

This is a wonderful dish to make from left-over chapatis. The corn and mushroom filling adds crunchiness to these rolls. Once you ensure that the chapattis are fat free and replace cheese with low fat cheese sauce, you have a 'heart friendly' dish at hand.

Preparation time : 15 minutes.   **Cooking time : 5 minutes.**   **Makes 4 rolls.**
Baking temperature : 220°C (430°F).   **Baking time : 15 to 20 minutes.**

4 left-over whole wheat chapatis, approximately 200 mm (8") in diameter

For the filling
½ cup corn kernels, boiled
½ cup tomatoes, blanched and chopped
½ cup mushrooms, chopped
¼ cup onions, chopped
½ teaspoon garlic, chopped
1 teaspoon dried oregano
1 teaspoon oil
salt to taste

For the mustard sauce
1 recipe low fat cheese sauce, page 133
½ teaspoon prepared mustard paste
salt to taste

For the filling
1. Heat the oil in a non-stick pan and add the onions, garlic and cook till the onions are translucent.
2. Add the tomatoes and mushrooms and cook for 2 to 3 minutes.
3. Add the corn kernels, oregano and salt and cook till the mixture is completely dry. Cool and keep aside.

For the mustard sauce
Mix all the ingredients together and keep aside.

How to proceed

1. Place one chapati on a dry surface and spread 2 tablespoons of the filling on one side. Roll up the chapati tightly.
2. Repeat to make 3 more roll ups.
3. Place the prepared roll ups on a greased baking dish and spoon the mustard sauce over them.
4. Bake in a pre-heated oven at 220°C (430°F) for 10 to 15 minutes. Serve hot.

Nutritive values per roll:

AMT	ENERGY	PROTEIN	CHO	FAT	FIBRE
gm	kcal	gm	gm	gm	gm
106	207	11.1	36.2	2.1	1.3

 Penne with Spinach in Low Fat Cheese Sauce

Penne tossed together with spinach and the low fat cheese sauce is sure to delight your palate. The cheese in this recipe has been replaced by low fat cottage cheese and so this main course with just 99 calories offers a guilt free meal for the healthy heart.

Preparation time : 10 minutes.   *Cooking time : 10 minutes.*   *Serves 2.*

1 cup penne, boiled
1 cup spinach (palak), blanched and chopped
¼ cup onions, chopped
1 teaspoon garlic, chopped
1 recipe low fat cheese sauce, page 133
a pinch nutmeg (jaiphal) powder
1 teaspoon oil or olive oil
salt to taste

1. Heat the oil in a non-stick pan, add the onions and garlic and cook till the onions are translucent.

2. Add the spinach and cook for another 2 to 3 minutes.
3. Add the penne, low fat cheese sauce, nutmeg powder and salt and allow it to come to a boil. Add some water if required, to adjust the consistency. Serve immediately.

Nutritive values per serving:

AMT	ENERGY	PROTEIN	CHO	FAT	FIBRE
gm	kcal	gm	gm	gm	gm
249	198	13.3	27.3	4.1	1.5

Full of Fibre Pasta

As the name suggests, this pasta is full of fibre. Use of whole-wheat pasta and lots of vegetables is the speciality of this fibre rich dish.

Preparation time : 10 minutes.   *Cooking time : 10 minutes.*   *Serves 2.*

For the sauce
½ cup onions, finely chopped
½ cup mixed vegetables (carrots, capsicum etc.) finely chopped
2 teaspoons garlic, finely chopped
½ cup low fat milk, page 130
1 teaspoon cornflour
1 teaspoon oil
salt and freshly ground pepper to taste

For the pasta
1½ cups whole wheat pasta, cooked
1 teaspoon garlic, finely chopped
1 dry red chilli
½ teaspoon oil

For the garnish
1 tablespoon finely chopped parsley

For the sauce

1. Heat the oil in a non-stick pan and add the onions.
2. Sauté the onions for 4 to 6 minutes till they are soft over a low flame.
3. Add the vegetables, garlic and salt and sauté again for 5 to 7 minutes.
4. Add ¼ cup water and cover and simmer till the vegetables are soft.
5. Add the milk and cornflour and mix well.
6. Bring to a boil, add the pepper and keep aside.

How to proceed

1. Heat the oil in a non-stick pan and add the garlic and red chilli and sauté for a few seconds.
2. Add the pasta and toss well.
3. Add the prepared sauce and mix well.
   Serve hot topped with the parsley.

Handy tip : You may use whole wheat fusilli, penne or tagliatelle.

Nutritive values per serving:

AMT	ENERGY	PROTEIN	CHO	FAT	FIBRE
gm	kcal	gm	gm	gm	gm
149	165	6.0	28.1	3.3	1.4

Paneer Shavarma Wrap

A serving of two of these wraps with a glass of Golden Glory Frappé, page 46, is good to satiate you at dinnertime and keep you going till the next morning. This meal is full of energy, fibre and flavour.

Preparation time : 15 minutes.   Cooking time : 15 minutes.   Makes 2 wraps.

For the paneer shavarma

½ cup low fat paneer (cottage cheese), page 132, diced
¼ cup onions, sliced
1 teaspoon cumin seeds (jeera)
¼ teaspoon cinnamon (dalchini) powder
½ teaspoon lemon juice

½ teaspoon honey
1 teaspoon green chillies, finely chopped
1 teaspoon oil
salt to taste

Other ingredients
2 chapatis (150 mm. (6") diameter)
¼ cup tomatoes, cut into thin strips
2 tablespoons mint, chopped
½ recipe herbed hummus, page 69

For the paneer shavarma
1. Grind together all the ingredients, other than the paneer and oil, into a smooth paste.
2. Apply the onion mixture on the paneer and keep aside.
3. Heat the oil in a non-stick pan and sauté the marinated paneer cubes, along with the paste for 2 to 3 minutes, till it turns golden in colour.
4. Turn the paneer cubes over and cook till the other side turns golden in colour.
5. Remove and keep aside.

How to proceed
1. Heat one chapati lightly on a pan and keep aside.
2. Apply half the hummus evenly on one side of the chapati, place half the paneer in the centre, sprinkle 1 tablespoon mint leaves and half the tomatoes and roll up the chapati.
3. Repeat with the second chapati to make one more wrap.
   Serve immediately.

Nutritive values per wrap:

AMT	ENERGY	PROTEIN	CHO	FAT	FIBRE
gm	kcal	gm	gm	gm	gm
118	181	11.2	27.5	3.2	1.4

Oatmeal and Spinach Crêpes

These crêpes are made healthy by the use of whole wheat flour instead of maida. Oats and spinach have been added to further enrich them with fibre. In the filling too, cheese has been substituted with veggies, excluding the fat component.

Preparation time : 20 minutes.   Cooking time: 25 minutes.   Makes 8 crêpes.
Baking time : 20 minutes.   Baking temperature : 230°C (450°F).

For the crêpes
¾ cup whole wheat flour (gehun ka atta)
¼ cup cornflour
3 tablespoons quick cooking rolled oats
2 cups spinach (palak), chopped
1 tablespoon oil
salt to taste

For the ratatouille stuffing
½ cup zucchini, finely chopped
½ cup brinjal, finely chopped
½ cup capsicum, finely chopped
½ cup onions, finely chopped
½ teaspoon finely chopped garlic
1 tablespoon finely chopped celery
½ cup tomatoes, finely chopped
½ teaspoon dried oregano
1 teaspoon oil
salt and pepper to taste

For baking
2½ cups low calorie white sauce, recipe below

For the low calorie white sauce
1½ cups cauliflower or bottle gourd (lauki / doodhi), chopped
1 tablespoon butter
1 tablespoon whole wheat flour (gehun ka atta)
1 cup low fat milk, page130
salt to taste
pepper to taste

For the low calorie white sauce
1. Boil the cauliflower in 2 cups of water until soft. Blend in a liquidiser and strain.
2. Heat the butter, add the whole wheat flour and sauté for a few seconds.
3. Add the milk and cauliflower purée and bring to a boil while stirring the mixture continuously till it becomes thick.
4. Add salt and pepper and bring to a boil. Keep aside.

For the crêpes
1. Blanch the spinach in hot water for a few seconds and immerse in cold water.
2. Drain and purée to a paste in a blender adding a little water if required.
3. Mix together all the ingredients with enough water to make a batter of coating consistency.
4. Heat a 6" diameter non-stick pan over medium flame and pour 3 tablespoons of batter onto the pan and move the pan in a circular motion, so as to spread the batter into a thin layer along the whole surface of the pan.
5. Cook over a medium flame till the crepe leaves the side of the pan. Remove and keep aside.
6. Repeat with the remaining batter to make 7 more crepes.

For the ratatouille stuffing
1. Heat the oil in a non-stick pan, add the zucchini, brinjal, capsicum, onions, garlic and celery and sauté for 2 minutes.
2. Add the tomatoes and salt and soak for 5 to 7 minutes the tomatoes and salt and cook for 5 to 7 minutes till the vegetables are soft.
3. Add the pepper and oregano and mix well. Allow it to cool.

How to proceed
1. Spoon out 1 portion of the stuffing onto the centre of each pancake, spread a little white sauce on top and roll up.
2. Arrange in a baking dish. Pour the remaining white sauce on top and bake in a hot oven at 230°C (450°F) for 20 minutes or until golden brown.
   Serve hot.

Nutritive values per crépe:

AMT	ENERGY	PROTEIN	CHO	FAT	FIBRE
gm	kcal	gm	gm	gm	gm
111	110	3.8	15.7	3.5	1.2

Whole Wheat Tagliatelle with Spinach Dumplings

The steamed spinach dumplings are usually served in a rich cheese sauce, almond sauce or butter sauce. For a healthy combination, this has been substituted with a low cal, yet creamy pumpkin sauce.
Make sure to add dal the dumplings and the sauce just before serving.

Preparation time : 20 minutes.   *Cooking time : 20 minutes.*   *Serves 2.*

For the tagliatelle
½ cup whole wheat flour (gehun ka atta)
1 teaspoon oil
salt to taste

For the pumpkin sauce
½ cup red pumpkin (kaddu), grated
¼ cup onions, chopped
¼ teaspoon garlic, chopped
¼ teaspoon dried thyme
½ teaspoon low fat butter
½ cup low fat milk, page 130
½ teaspoon dry red chilli flakes

For the spinach dumplings
1 cup spinach (palak), blanched and chopped
½ cup low fat paneer (cottage cheese), page 132, grated
a pinch nutmeg (jaiphal) powder
salt to taste

Other ingredients
1 teaspoon of oil for cooking

For the tagliatelle
1. Mix all the ingredients together and using enough water make a form dough.
2. Cover the dough with a wet muslin cloth and keep aside for 10 to 15 minutes.
3. Divide the dough into 2 equal portions and roll out each portion, using a little flour for dusting, to a (175 mm) 7" diameter circle.

4. Using a knife or a pizza cutter, cut into long strips which are 6 mm. (¼") broad.
5. Dust a plate with some flour and place the strips on the dusted plate.
6. Boil plenty of water in a large pot and add one teaspoon oil and 2 teaspoons salt.
7. Add ½ the tagliatelle to the boiling water and cook till it floats (approx. 1 minute).
8. Remove the cooked tagliatelle with a sieve and place them in cold water.
9. Drain and discard the water and keep the tagliatelle aside.
10. Repeat with remaining half tagliatelle.
11. Add 1 teaspoon oil to the cooked pasta, toss gently and keep covered.

For the pumpkin sauce
1. Heat the butter in a non-stick pan, add the onions, garlic and thyme and cook till the onions turn translucent.
2. Add the pumpkin and cook for 3 to 4 minutes till the pumpkin is tender.
3. Cool the mixture and blend in a mixer to a smooth purée.
4. Heat the purée in a pan, add milk, red chilli flakes and salt and allow the mixture to come to a boil. Keep aside.

For the spinach dumplings
Mix all the ingredients shape into small balls and keep aside.

How to proceed
1. Heat the pumpkin sauce in a pan, add the tagliatelle and mix well.
2. Spoon out the tagliatelle into a serving dish, place the spinach dumplings on top and serve immediately.

Handy tip : The pumpkin sauce can be substituted with low calorie white sauce, page 116, if you so desire.

Nutritive values per serving:

AMT	ENERGY	PROTEIN	CHO	FAT	FIBRE
gm	kcal	gm	gm	gm	gm
81	150	4.2	22.4	4.8	0.8

Custard Fruit Tarts

The custard fruit tarts are made with low fat butter, minimal sugar and fruits like oranges and strawberry to make your dessert full of fibre. The custard too makes use of low fat milk and just a tablespoon of sugar. Enjoy this low cal version of fruit tarts as an occasional sumptuous treat.

Preparation time : 15 minutes. *Cooking time : 10 minutes.* *Makes 8 tarts.*
Baking temperature : 180°C (360°F). *Baking time : 15 minutes.*

For the tarts
2 teaspoons low fat butter
1 tablespoon castor sugar
¾ cup plain flour (maida)
a pinch baking powder
1 tablespoon custard powder

For the low fat custard
1 cup low fat milk, page 130
1 tablespoon custard powder
1 tablespoon sugar
½ teaspoon vanilla essence

Other ingredients
½ teaspoon oil for greasing
plain flour (maida) for dusting

For the garnish
8 kiwi slices
8 strawberry slices
8 orange segments

For the tarts
1. Sieve together the flour and baking powder.
2. Cream the low fat butter and sugar in a bowl with a wooden spoon till light and fluffy.

3. Add the flour and custard powder in 2 batches and mix lightly to form a dough.
4. Knead the dough on a light dusted surface until smooth.
5. Divide the dough into 8 equal portions.
6. Press each portion into greased tart moulds (approx. 25 mm. (1") diameter).
7. Prick with a fork.
8. Bake in a pre-heated oven at 180°F (360°F) for 15 minutes or until the tarts are golden in colour.
9. Remove, unmould and cool. Store in an air-tight container.

For the custard
1. Mix the custard powder in ¼ cup milk and keep aside.
2. Heat the remaining milk with the sugar and mix well.
3. Add the custard powder mixture and vanilla essence and cook over a low flame, stirring continuously till the mixture coats the back of the spoon.
4. Cool and keep aside.

How to proceed
1. Fill the tarts with the custard, and refrigerate until the custard is set.
2. Serve garnished with slices of kiwi, strawberry and orange segments.

Nutritive values per tart:

AMT	ENERGY	PROTEIN	CHO	FAT	FIBRE
gm	kcal	gm	gm	gm	gm
42	83	2.4	16.1	0.8	0.3

Lauki ki Kheer

You all must have enjoyed the traditional Indian kheer. Now try this traditional recipe in my healthy way to satisfy your sweet tooth. The recipe makes use of fibre rich doodhi and low fat milk and milk powder, which is easily available to all the grocery stores.

Preparation time : 10 minutes.   *Cooking time : 20 minutes.*   *Serves 4.*

1 cup bottle gourd (doodhi/lauki), grated
2 cups low fat milk, page 130
2 tablespoons skim milk powder

2 tablespoons sugar
½ teaspoon cardamom (elaichi) powder

1. Combine the bottle gourd, milk and milk powder in a non-stick pan and
    simmer for 10 to 15 minutes till the bottle gourd is cooked.
2. Add the sugar and cook till the sugar dissolves.
3. Add the cardamom powder, mix well and refrigerate.
    Serve chilled.

Nutritive values per serving:

AMT	ENERGY	PROTEIN	CHO	FAT	FIBRE
gm	kcal	gm	gm	gm	gm
48	90	6.1	16.2	0.0	0.1

 Baked Cottage Cheese Pie

One of my favourite desserts which tastes delicious when it is served.
warm.
Made just with low fat paneer and fruits, you can occasionally enjoy a
serving of this dessert after your meal. However, do remember to include
these calories as part of your diet.

Preparation time : 10 minutes.   *Baking time: 15 minutes.*   *Serves 4.*
                                          Baking temperature : 220°C (440°F).

For the cottage cheese mixture
1 cup low fat paneer (cottage cheese), page 132
4 teaspoons sugar
4 tablespoons low fat milk, page 130
a few strands of saffron

For the fruit filling
1 cup apples, sliced
4 teaspoons brown sugar
¼ teaspoon nutmeg (jaiphal) powder
a few drops lemon juice

For the cottage cheese mixture
1. Dissolve the saffron in the milk and keep aside
2. Blend together all the ingredients in a blender to a smooth paste. Keep aside.

For the fruit filling
1. Mix together all the ingredients and keep aside for 15 to 20 minutes.
2. Squeeze out all the water and arrange the fruit in a greased 150 mm. (6") diameter pie dish.

How to proceed
Spread the cottage cheese mixture over the fruit and bake in a pre-heated oven at 220°C (440°F) for 15 minutes.
Serve warm.

Nutritive values per serving:

AMT	ENERGY	PROTEIN	CHO	FAT	FIBRE
gm	kcal	gm	gm	gm	gm
62	132	8.8	23.8	0.2	0.3

 # Date and Walnut Footballs

This is a completely fuss-free delicacy, not too high in calories as this delicacy is completely devoid of sugar. Instead dates have been added, as they contain plenty of fibre and natural sugar, while walnuts are rich in linoleic acid which have been proven to be helpful to strengthen the arteries of the heart.

Preparation time : a few minutes. **No cooking.** **Makes 8 footballs.**

½ cup black seedless dates
2 tablespoons walnuts, toasted
¼ teaspoon cardamom (elaichi) powder

1. Knead the dates into a smooth dough.
2. Add the walnuts and cardamom powder and mix well.
3. Divide the mixture into 8 portions and shape into balls.
   Serve at room temperature.

AMT	ENERGY	PROTEIN	CHO	FAT	FIBRE
gm	kcal	gm	gm	gm	gm
13	39	0.7	3.6	2.5	0.4

Apricot Stew with Vanilla Custard

Warm smooth apricots, topped with low fat chilled custard and garnished with almonds — this mouth-watering dessert is one of the best sweets that a person with hyped cholesterol level can enjoy. Apricots are rich in sweetness, so restrict the addition of sugar to just 3 teaspoons for a twin serving.

Preparation time : 10 minutes.   **Cooking time : 20 minutes.**   *Serves 2.*

For the stew
1½ cups dried apricots
2 sticks cinnamon (dalchini)
1 clove (laung)
juice of ½ lemon

For the vanilla custard
1 cup low fat milk, page 130
2 teaspoons vanilla custard powder
3 teaspoons sugar

For the garnish
2 teaspoons chopped walnuts

For the stew
1. Soak the apricots in 1 cup of hot water for approx. 3 to 4 hours.
2. Deseed and add all the other ingredients and allow the water to come to a boil.
3. Simmer over medium flame for 5 minutes, till the apricots are soft and syrupy.

For the vanilla custard
1. Mix the custard powder in ¼ cup milk and keep aside.
2. Boil the remaining milk with the sugar, add the custard powder mixture and cook over a slow flame till the custard coats the back of a spoon. Cool and keep aside.

How to proceed
1. Place half the stewed apricots in a serving bowl and pour half the chilled custard over the apricots.
2. Repeat to make another serving. Serve garnished with the walnuts.

Nutritive values per serving:

AMT	ENERGY	PROTEIN	CHO	FAT	FIBRE
gm	kcal	gm	gm	gm	gm
30	70	1.4	9.3	3.0	0.2

Soya Date Cookies

So simple, yet so delicious!! Cookies made with healthy ingredients like soya flour and dates are simply irresistible. The soya helps to decrease bad cholesterol (LDL) level is the body while the dates act as a healthy substitute for sugar. Enjoy these guilt free goodies any time of the day.

Preparation time : 10 minutes.   **Baking time : 25 minutes.**   **Makes 12 cookies.**
Baking temperature : 180°C (360°F).

For the date purée
¼ cup dates deeseded

For the dough
¼ cup soya flour
¼ cup whole wheat flour (gehun ka atta)
¼ cup low fat butter
2 tablespoons sugar

For the date purée
1. Chop the dates into small pieces and add ½ cup of water.
2. Bring to a boil in a non-stick pan and simmer for 10 to 12 minutes till the dates are fully mashed into a purée.
3. Cool and keep aside.

For the dough
1. Combine the whole wheat flour, butter and sugar in a bowl using your fingertips till the mixture resembles bread crumbs.
2. Add the cooled date purée and knead it into a dough.
3. Cover with a plastic film and refrigerate for 15 minutes.
4. Roll out into a sheet of 6 mm. (¼") thickness and cut out cookies approx. 37 mm. (1½") in diameter using a cookie cutter.
5. Re-roll the scraps of dough to make more cookies and place them on a baking tray (line the cookie sheet with greased proof paper).
6. Bake in a pre-heated oven at 180ºC (360ºF) for 25 minutes or till the cookies are golden brown.
7. Cool and store in an air-tight container.

Nutritive values per cookie :

AMT	ENERGY	PROTEIN	CHO	FAT	FIBRE
gm	kcal	gm	gm	gm	gm
13	52	1.3	5.9	2.5	0.2

Soya Nankhatai

A sweet treat that's good for your heart. Soya flour has been used to give it a healthy touch as it helps in decreasing bad cholesterol (LDL) while building up good cholesterol (HDL). Make these healthy delicacies in advance and serve them to your guests too!

Preparation time : 10 minutes.   Baking time : 25 to 30 minutes.   Makes 20 nankhatais.
Baking temperature : 140°C (280°F).

½ cup soya flour
½ cup whole wheat flour (gehun ka atta)
¼ teaspoon soda bi-carb
1 tablespoon low fat curds, page 131
2 tablespoons powdered sugar
¼ teaspoon nutmeg (jaiphal) powder
¼ teaspoon cardamom (elaichi) powder
1 tablespoon softened low fat butter
1 tablespoon oil
a pinch salt

Other ingredients
1 teaspoon oil for greasing

1. Combine all the ingredients in a bowl and mix well using your fingertips till they resemble breadcrumbs.
2. Add approx. 2 tablespoons of cold water and knead it gently into a crumbly dough.
3. Divide into 20 equal portions. Roll into a ball and flatten between your palms.
4. Place them on a lightly greased baking tray.
5. Bake in a pre-heated oven at 140°C (280°F) for 25 to 30 minutes or till they are golden brown.
6. Cool and store in an air-tight container.

Nutritive values per nankhatai:

AMT	ENERGY	PROTEIN	CHO	FAT	FIBRE
gm	kcal	gm	gm	gm	gm
8	35	1.1	3.8	1.7	0.1

Bulgur Wheat Kheer

Kheer is one of the favourite Indian desserts that is irresistible. Unfortunately, traditionally kheer is laden with fat and calories due to addition of high amounts of sugar, nuts and full fat milk. This version makes use of high fibre bulgur wheat, low fat milk and just a tablespoon of sugar per serving.

Preparation time : 15 minutes.   *Cooking time : 15 minutes.*   *Serves 2.*

¼ cup bulgur wheat (dalia)
1½ cups low fat milk, page 130
½ teaspoon cardamom (elaichi) powder
2 tablespoons sugar
a few strands saffron

For the garnish
1 to 2 rose petals, shredded

1. Wash and soak the bulgur wheat in ½ cup water for 15 to 20 minutes.
2. Drain and discard the water and cook the soaked bulgur wheat with 1 cup water.
3. When the water evaporates, add the milk and sugar and allow the mixture to come to a boil. Remove and allow it to cool.
4. Dissolve saffron in 2 tablespoons milk and add the saffron and cardamom powder to the cooked mixture and mix well. Serve chilled garnished with the shredded rose petals.

Nutritive values per serving:

AMT	ENERGY	PROTEIN	CHO	FAT	FIBRE
gm	kcal	gm	gm	gm	gm
49	180	7.2	6.9	0.3	0.3

Fig and Cardamom Delight

This sumptuous, easy-to-make, sweet dish can be made in advance and refrigerated. Figs have been used as they are low in calories as compared to other dried fruits and are also rich in fibre. To control the calorie count further, I have used skim milk and restricted the sugar to minimal.

Preparation time: 15 minutes.   *Cooking time : 10 minutes.*   *Makes 4 glasses.*

½ packet (5 grams) agar-agar, chopped
2½ cups low fat milk, page 130
3 teaspoons skim milk powder
3 teaspoons sugar
2 pinches cardamom (elaichi) powder
2 pinches saffron
8 dried figs, soaked in ½ cup water and puréed

1. Mix the milk with the milk powder and keep aside..
2. Add ¾ cup water to the agar-agar and simmer over a slow flame till it melts.
3. Add the milk mixture, sugar, cardamom powder, fig purée and mix well.
4. Pour into individual glasses and refrigerate till it sets.

Nutritive values per glass:

AMT	ENERGY	PROTEIN	CHO	FAT	FIBRE
gm	kcal	gm	gm	gm	gm
31	66	5.1	11.4	0.0	0.3

BASIC RECIPES

Low Fat Milk

The low fat milk, made by using skimmed milk powder, has the all the goodness of milk like protein, calcium and vitamin B₂, but is virtually fat free. Skim milk powder is easily available at all leading grocery stores. Alternatively, you can use 99% fat free milk (low fat milk), readily available in tetra packs in the market. This low fat milk gives you only 71 calories per cup in comparison to 234 calories available per cup, coupled with 13 grams of fat available from full fat milk.

Preparation time : 5 minutes.   *Cooking time : 7 minutes.*   *Makes 1 litre (5 cups).*

100 grams skim milk powder
1 litre water

1. Mix the skim milk powder in 1½ cups of water and make a smooth paste.
2. Add the remaining water and if desired, mix with a whisk.
3. Boil and use as required.

Note : Different packets of skim milk have different methods of preparation. The above procedure has been given for your guidance and the instructions on the packet should be followed.

Nutritive values per cup:

AMT	ENERGY	PROTEIN	CHO	FAT	FIBRE
gm	kcal	gm	gm	gm	gm
200	71	7.6	10.2	0.0	0.0

Low Fat Curds

Curds are a wholesome and nourishing addition to your diet. They are easier to digest than milk, and when accompanied with dishes like parathas, biryanis etc., curds complement the protein present in cereals and make it a complete protein.

Use this low fat version of curds as an accompaniment to the main meal or in raitas, salad dressings etc., to enjoy a delightful low calorie fare.

Preparation time: 5 minutes. *Setting time : 6 hours..* *Makes 5 cups.*

1 litre low fat milk, page 130
1 tablespoon curds (made the previous day)

1. Warm the milk.
2. Add the curds, mix well and cover.
3. Keep aside until the curds set (approximately 5 to 6 hours). During the cold climate, place inside a cupboard or closed oven to set.

Nutritive values per cup:

AMT	ENERGY	PROTEIN	CHO	FAT	FIBRE
gm	kcal	gm	gm	gm	gm
200	71	7.6	10.2	0.0	0.0

Low Fat Paneer

This paneer is prepared from low fat milk that has all the goodness of milk without its fat content. For milk fussy adults, this is a superb way of adding protein (necessary for maintenance of body cells) and calcium (necessary for healthy bones) to the diet. Making snacks, subzis, desserts etc. with this low fat paneer is a ladder to a hearty meal.

Preparation time : 30 minutes.   Cooking time : 10 minutes.   Makes 100 grams. (approx. ¾ cup).

2 cups low fat milk, page 130
1 cup low fat curds, page 131, beaten

1. Put the milk to boil in a broad pan. When it starts boiling, add the low fat curds and mix well.
2. Remove from the heat and stir gently until the milk curdles.
3. Strain, tie the curdled milk in a muslin cloth and hang for about ½ hour to allow the whey to drain out.
4. Use as required.

Handy Tip :
If the milk has not curdled completely in step 2, cook the mixture a little longer.

Nutritive values per 100 grams:

AMT	ENERGY	PROTEIN	CHO	FAT	FIBRE
gm	kcal	gm	gm	gm	gm
100	214	22.8	30.6	0.1	0.0

Low Fat Cheese Sauce

This is used as a substitute for cheese in most baked dishes like Baked Vegetable Roll Up, page 109, or pastas like Penne with Spinach in Low Fat Cheese Sauce, page 110. Be sure to make fresh sauce each time you need to use it. The sauce is prepared from low fat dairy products like milk and paneer, so doesn't abound in fat and doesn't contribute excess calories to the diet of people with heart problems.

Preparation time : 15 minutes.   *Cooking time : 5 minutes.*   *Makes 1 cup.*

1 cup low fat milk, page 130
½ cup low fat paneer, page 132, crumbled

1. Blend the ingredients together to make a smooth sauce.
2. Bring to a boil and use as required.

Nutritive values for 1 cup:

AMT	ENERGY	PROTEIN	CHO	FAT	FIBRE
gm	kcal	gm	gm	gm	gm
63	235	239	32.1	2.1	1.3

Sample Breakfast Menus

MENU	AMOUNT	ENERGY (kcal)	PROTEIN (gm)	CHO (gm)	FAT (gm)	FIBRE (gm)
Carrot Coriander Juice, page 44	1 serving	30	0.6	0.4	0.2	0.8
Sprouted Moong and Methi Chilas, page 41	3 nos.	252	13.4	33.5	6.8	2.4
Papaya, sliced	1 cup	45	0.8	10.5	0.1	1.7
TOTAL		327	14.8	50.4	7.1	4.9

MENU	AMOUNT	ENERGY (kcal)	PROTEIN (gm)	CHO (gm)	FAT (gm)	FIBRE (gm)
Whole Wheat Salad Wrap, page 39	2 nos.	224	12.0	34.2	4.4	3.4
Orange	1 cup, segmented	84	1.2	19.2	0.4	0.5
TOTAL		308	13.2	53.4	4.8	3.9

Sample Snack Menus

MENU	AMOUNT	ENERGY (kcal)	PROTEIN (gm)	CHO (gm)	FAT (gm)	FIBRE (gm)
Soya Bhel, page 65	1 serving	83	8.0	4.9	3.5	1.0
Apple	1 no.	124	0.4	28.1	1.1	2.1
TOTAL		207	8.4	33.0	4.6	3.1

MENU	AMOUNT	ENERGY (kcal)	PROTEIN (gm)	CHO (gm)	FAT (gm)	FIBRE (gm)
Waldorf Open Sandwich, page 43	1 sandwich	165	8.2	31.5	0.8	1.8
Golden Glory Frappé, page 46	1 serving	72	1.7	15.9	0.3	1.2
TOTAL		237	9.9	47.4	1.1	3.0

Sample Lunch Menus

MENU	AMOUNT	ENERGY (kcal)	PROTEIN (gm)	CHO (gm)	FAT (gm)	FIBRE (gm)
Makai Shorba, page 50	1 serving	69	1.5	11.0	2.6	1.1
Whole Wheat Phulkas	3 nos.	153	5.4	31.2	0.8	0.9
Pyazwali Bhindi, page 88	1 serving	120	4.0	14.4	5.2	1.2
Chick Pea and Mint Rice, page 107	1 serving	199	5.1	39.9	2.1	0.9
Lauki ki Kheer, page 121	1 serving	90	6.1	16.2	0.0	0.1
TOTAL		631	22.1	112.7	10.7	4.2

MENU	AMOUNT	ENERGY (kcal)	PROTEIN (gm)	CHO (gm)	FAT (gm)	FIBRE (gm)
Garlic Vegetable Soup, page 48	1 serving	49	1.6	7.5	1.5	0.9
Oriental Soya and Babycorn Stir-fry, page 58	1 serving	129	6.8	16.9	3.6	2.1
Oatmeal and Spinach Crêpes, page 116	2 crêpes	220	7.6	31.4	7.1	2.3
Bulgur Wheat Salad, page 75	1 serving	83	2.9	17.1	0.4	0.7
Apple	1 no.	124	0.4	28.1	1.1	2.1
TOTAL		605	19.3	101.0	13.7	8.1

Sample Dinner Menus

MENU	AMOUNT	ENERGY (kcal)	PROTEIN (gm)	CHO (gm)	FAT (gm)	FIBRE (gm)
Oat and Spring Onion Paratha, page 97	1 no.	117	3.9	19.8	2.6	1.1
Lauki Kofta Curry, page 81	1 serving	65	3.1	13.6	2.0	0.8
Cabbage Pulao, page 106	1 serving	175	4.9	31.4	3.3	0.7
Carrot and Mint Salad, page 74	1 serving	165	7.1	33.6	0.7	2.9
Pineapple, chopped	1 cup	76	0.7	17.9	0.2	0.8
TOTAL		**619**	**19.8**	**116.7**	**8.7**	**6.2**

MENU	AMOUNT	ENERGY (kcal)	PROTEIN (gm)	CHO (gm)	FAT (gm)	FIBRE (gm)
Spinach Soup with Garlic, page 57	1 serving	37	1.3	4.2	1.6	0.5
Crunchy Cumin Seed Crackers, page 61	5 nos.	89	3.5	15.2	1.6	0.5
Sweet Potato Salad, page 78	1 serving	175	3.4	16.3	10.8	1.3
Full of Fibre Pasta, page 113	1 tarts	165	6.0	28.1	3.3	1.4
Baked Cottage Cheese Pie, page 122	1 serving	132	8.8	23.8	0.2	0.3
Papaya, sliced	1 cup	45	0.8	10.5	0.1	1.7
TOTAL		**643**	**23.8**	**98.1**	**17.6**	**5.7**